BOOK WORKS

NORTHERN LINE

Bon jour! This is graphite the miner
follow this line of words I am drawing
using the logical cartography wherein
paper were the Earth the Sun would c

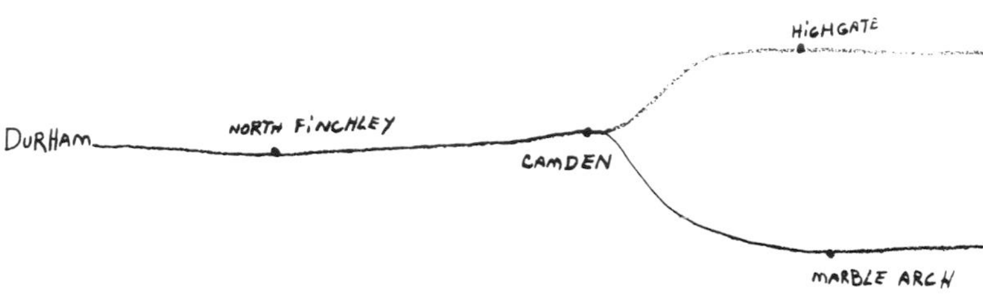

Above: *Northern Line.* Jimmie Durham, unique graphite text drawing from the limited edition version of *East London Coelacanth*, published by Book Works and the ICA (1993-94)
Inside cover: Performance by Chris Newman at launch of *Me*, Serpentine Gallery, London, (1993)
Previous page: Book Works, Holywell Row (1996)

BOOK WORKS
A PARTIAL HISTORY AND SOURCEBOOK

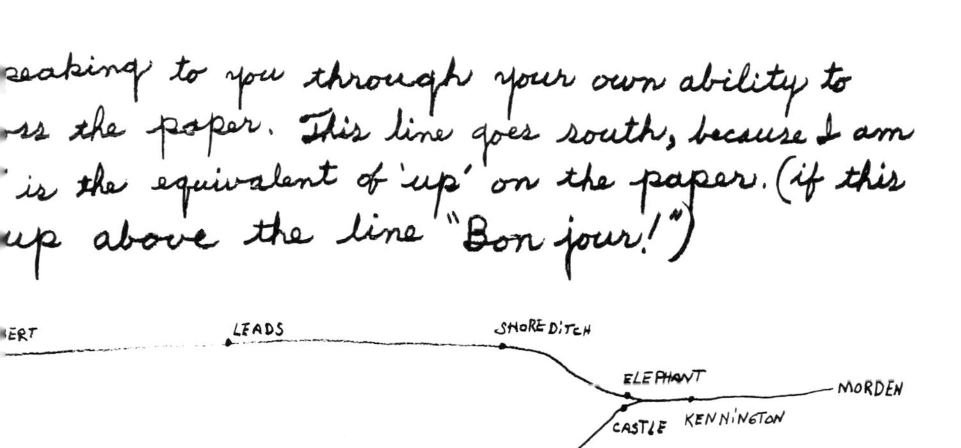

Edited by Jane Rolo and Ian Hunt

Book Works 1996

BOOK WORKS

A PARTIAL HISTORY AND SOURCEBOOK

Edited by Jane Rolo and Ian Hunt

Book Works would like to acknowledge financial support from the
Arts Council of England and the London Arts Board

Published and distributed by Book Works
19 Holywell Row
London EC2A 4JB

Designed and Typeset by John & Orna Designs
Printed by Balding + Mansell, Kettering
Edition: 2,000
ISBN 1 870699 20 3

CONTENTS

Indian Children

& PERPLEXITY
UNTIL THE BISHOPS OPEN
Of Sealed Writings
THE PANACEA SOCIETY
BEDFORD, ENGLAND
ACHERON
LETHE
MNEMOSYNE

Previous pages: *Susan Hiller at the Freud Museum*. Susan Hiller, installation as part of *The Reading Room*, Freud Museum, London (1994), boxes, artefacts, and labels

This book is a testament to the collaborations that have taken place at Book Works, recording the exhibitions and events that have happened and the new work that has been made with many different artists. The emphasis of the kind of work produced may have shifted over time, but our aim remains to commission and produce new work in full collaboration with artists, whether it be publishing and producing books, multiples, videos, and CD-Roms or realising installations, time-based or performance works, or inaugurating discussions. Equally important to us is the dissemination of the work, and the relationship of the work to a potential audience, and the context and place that a particular work might occupy. The visual arts arena, which has been changing fast in Britain since we set out, is clearly the context but in various ways the examination of the continuing importance of the book, its form and its content, has provided us with a flexible framework for intervening. To state in the abstract how politics inform the choices we've made would be difficult, but we hope it's clear that they're there, aided by the peculiar fact that the symbolic power of the book keeps its ability to focus artists on what they consider most urgent to communicate. Even if that something urgent turns out to be something that at first sight seems light-hearted.

We hope this book will offer an insight into how Book Works' activities have developed over the years and be a useful resource and inspiration to others. There are of course many reference books, catalogues and articles about artists' books and their history, and numerous definitions, surveys and lists that make fascinating reading, and although this book makes no excuses for the fact that it concentrates on the activities of Book Works, some general reference must be made to the context within which we see our work existing.

Artists' books are not conventional in terms of content. They are not books about artists or their work, but exist as the works in their own right. Although their form may seem familiar, in that they often have a sequence of pages, held together at the spine, the information contained inside does not necessarily follow a formula, and may actively seek to disrupt habitual or familiar ways of seeing and reading. People often speak of 'reading' works of art: artists' books ask the reader to read words, pictures, intervals and other factors such as format and typography. This does not mean artists' books are necessarily disruptive. Sometimes they are contemplative, and sometimes they are happy to take the conventional written forms of the story, poem, diary or anthology — though often to claim them for content that has been overlooked. The relationship between these books and the reader, and how the physical environment of the space that a book creates and occupies can alter one's perception or 'reading' of the book is central to Book Works' philosophy of commissioning and publishing new work.

The book is perhaps still the most intimate, easily accessible and portable of art forms, and thus sets up an easy dialogue between author and reader. Many artists' books are however by necessity presented formally to the reader, as if they were museum objects, and thus must be read in a certain way.

Representing the various activities between 1984 and 1996, this book will show some of Book Works' involvement with producing and publishing artists' books. Book Works makes work in collaboration with an artist and is usually involved from the initial ideas through to the final stages of production. The books may combine texts with image to explore a wide range of subjects and methods of printing and binding.

Unlike a writer's page, the artist's page may be treated as an empty canvas. The work considers the physical properties as well as the content or communication of ideas. The reader is invited to enter into different worlds through the pages of the book. Taken a stage further, these books can often be seen in the context of related events: performances, readings, sound works and installations.

The style and content of these books often merge to form an alternative reading experience, one that is not necessarily linear, where the artist sets the pace of 'reading'. In turn, the reader is encouraged to participate in an imaginative way.[1] Artists' books are comparable to the new hypertexts, where the reader is invited to 'interact' with the text, to transform it, modify it, and to create different experiences, but their modesty as well as their occasional lavishness makes for a quite distinct form of attention.

Artists' books have exploited an inexhausible range of contemporary materials, mixing traditional craftsmanship and technology in single forms. The synthesis of other forms of artistic expression present in artists' books breaks down barriers that exist between the various media, and which are often mutually antipathetic: the artist's book becomes a space for writing, painting and poetry, though it transforms the usual conventions of assimilating them. Along with the advent of each new technology and the wide variety of commercial printing techniques, the book's format and presentation may change, ensuring there will still be a role for the 'book' as a vehicle to communicate ideas.

The texts in this book offer different insights: Pavel Büchler positions the artist's book within an historical perspective uniquely his own, whilst Ann Gallagher gives a personal view of how she relates to the phenomenon of artists' books, and Michael Bracewell, the novelist and co-editor of our New Writing series, has written about his involvement with *The Reading Room* and on the sometimes vexed relationship between writing and art in the British context. Some other original texts are also included in the context of various projects.

1. *'Book art can be seen as an art of action, a kind of happening or theatre, concerned with the situation in which the work is experienced, and which demands the reader's participation. The book of course remains at the centre of such a situation, but the experience of the situation itself is controlled by the reader. . .'*

Pavel Büchler, *Turning Over the Pages: Some Books in Contemporary Art* (Cambridge: Kettle's Yard Gallery, 1986)

BOOKS AS BOOKS[1]

PAVEL BÜCHLER

'The artist's book is/was a great idea whose time has either not come, or come and gone', wrote Lucy Lippard, a long time supporter and promoter of the genre, in 1983.[2] But could it have been any other way?

'The central question,' says Lippard, 'revolves around function, and the role of art in general.' Indeed, it was the dissatisfaction with the role assigned to art under modernism, and the belief that artists could no longer pay for the privilege of maintaining a critical distance by having no means by which to affect society directly — that art could no longer legitimate its separation from a broader revolutionary praxis — that led to the early avant-garde's experimentation with the possibilities of publishing. From the Futurist Manifesto, published on the front page of *Le Figaro* in 1909, to the last issue of *Internationale Situationniste* of 1969, and the publications of Fluxus of the same era, newspapers, magazines, pamphlets and posters became the front lines of the battle for regaining a direct social and political role for art.

However, unlike newspapers, magazines and journals, whose periodicity seemed to be suited to the demands of the continuous flux of revolutionary rhetorics, and unlike leaflets or posters, whose ephemerality seemed to resent commodification and absorption into the drifts of merchandise, the book was far too firmly embedded in the tradition of permanence to provide an adequate vehicle for the avant-garde's intents and ideals. It belonged to the world of collectable commodities on the one hand, and to the realm of literature on the other — too closely tied to precisely those conditions of modern culture which the early historical avant-gardes sought to challenge.

It was not until the 1960s that the 'great idea' of the book as art emerged. The necessary precondition was the concept of the 'dematerialisation' of the art object — separation of the 'art' from the 'object' — which, at first, seemed to revolutionise the established functions of art.

With hindsight, however, it seems that by the 1960s all realistic possibility of a radical political and social change on which the avant-garde had based its beliefs had diminished in the western world, and the avant-garde project had to be left incomplete. The concept of 'dematerialisation' of the art object became a final retreat rather than a final victory. The decline of the avant-garde position is implied in the gradual shift of attention from the ephemeral publications — magazines, posters, pamphlets — to the more permanent and private aspects of books. For the artists of the subsequent generations, bringing books to the service of art (rather than bringing art to the service of books) meant precisely rejecting the revolutionary orthodoxies of the historical avant-gardes and reclaiming lost territories and, in particular, renewing visual art's 'old' links to language.

It could be argued that it was already the very invention of the letterpress in the mid-fifteenth century which gave rise to those conditions under which artistic production has been separated from the reality of consumption and social exchange. The 'Gutenberg revolution' marked the beginning of the mechanical era in which the printed book brought with itself an enormous potential for the commodification of thought, bringing literature into the bookshop and the supermarket, while sending art on its way from the public space of the cathedral into the privacy of the museum or the gallery. (The museum and the artist's studio are the monastery and the scriptorium of modernity!) In this context, the strategy of 'dematerialisation' of the art object does not appear confrontational. Rather, it seems to be aimed, primarily, at creating or re-establishing a new autonomy for the 'artwork' in the conditions of the end of the industrial age.

The philosophy and ideology of 'dematerialised' art provided the opportunity to explore the possibilities of the form of the book for the first time without sacrificing the integrity of the artistic gesture. The book as a work of conceptual art was neither a book as an object-commodity, nor was it a container for a content in the literary tradition. Yet, if it were to become a conceptually whole 'work' it could no longer remain 'just a book' either.

The rejection of the object in favour of process, idea or information also meant the abolition, for practical purposes, of the definition of a work of art based on the classical art historical categories of painting, sculpture and architecture. For a while, it seemed that anything could be the material pretext for a work of art as long as it was not something else at the same time. And for a thing which is neither a painting nor a sculpture, to be a work of art and not to be anything else at the same time meant simply not to be the thing itself.

It was felt by many contemporary commentators that new categories had to be defined. The generic term 'artist's book' was itself highly problematic. The expression, derived from the French *livre d'artiste*, formerly denoted books illustrated or designed by distinguished painters or craftsmen and usually produced in limited editions. In the 1960s it was to be used as a designation for often mass-produced books entirely made (in a conceptual sense) by artists. Furthermore, despite the marginal role that it had played among the media of the previous generations of avant-garde artists and poets, by the 1960s the book in art was not an entirely virgin territory and it was necessary to categorise the relationship between the book as an object and the conceptual idea of the book. Categories for different aspects or the book and for different ways in which the book could be used proliferated. Ulises Carrión described his Archive as a 'space for exhibition and distribution of other books, non books, anti books, pseudo books, quasi books, concrete books, conceptual books, structural books, project books, plain books . . .'; Hubert Kretschmer distinguished between 'Kunstlerbücher', 'Objektbücher' and 'Buchobjekte'; while Paul-Armand Gette came up with 'book-object-book' and 'object-book-object'. In 1975 Clive Phillpot drew a distinction between 'artists' books' and 'book art' and in 1982 he sub-divided 'book art' into 'book objects' and 'bookworks'. Three years later an authoritative survey at the Centre Georges Pompidou in Paris was organised in two sections, 'The book as support' and 'The book as an object', divided into no less than seventeen categories from 'Books of concrete and visual poetry' to 'Manuscript books and painting books' (with an extra category for those that don't fall into any of the previous ones and hence are 'Not a book').[3] To classify 'artists' books' (or 'books by artists', or 'books as art'), these and many other authors employed diverse criteria. Some would distinguish between various methods of production and distribution, whereas others would classify the books according to their contents, subject matter or style, or according to the extent to which they were a self-reflection of the nature and history of the book itself.

Clearly, the differentiation between 'artists' books' and other books sought not only to map the newly discovered conceptual possibilities, but also to re-accommodate the art object as a primary concern of visual art. By implication, the purpose of the new terminology was to establish critical independence which would, make it impossible to apply outside criteria to the books made by artists, i.e. to see 'artists' books' as books. The urgent need felt by so many to streamline books as art into categories also indicates the limitations of the 'great idea' of the book as art. If, as a genre, the artist's book failed to affect the function and role of art, as it had initially promised, it may well be not because it came too late or too early, but because it never came to terms with the book as simply a book.

'What is a book?' asks Ulises Carrión in his essay, *The New Art of Making Books*, first published in 1975.[4] 'A book is a sequence of spaces' and since 'each of these spaces is perceived at a different moment, a book is also a sequence of moments'; it is an 'autonomous space-time sequence', answers Carrión in the same text. The basic unit of a book is the double page; but one double page, a sheet of paper folded in half, is not yet a book. It is only through the repetition of the units that the sequence is established. A number of double pages bound together form the space of the book. A book is also a space-time whole. The sequence of spaces within a book is fixed and finite: it has a beginning and an end. Nothing can be added or taken without the book changing as a result. (A book with a page torn out is already a different book!) The completeness of the whole and its indivisibility are the essential features of the book. They provide the context and the frame for the book's content.

The content of the book is contained within the volume of the book. This is obviously true of a book whose content is the book itself, its own structure, but it is equally true of any other book. Elements or blocks of the content — both identical with the elements of the book and independent from them, texts, images or whatever — are organised within the space of the book. The relationships between them are spatial rather than linear. The content of the book is organised simultaneously in space.

It is perceived consecutively in time. While the structuring of the space is done by the maker of the book, the time sequence is only realised in the process of reading. It is the reader who chooses where to start and where to stop, how and what to read, how fast or how attentively. It is he or she who is turning over the pages. Guided or confronted by its structure, the reader manipulates the book — and through the interaction between the book and the reader, the content of the book reveals itself.

From this point of view 'book art' can be seen as an art of action, a kind of happening or event, concerned with the situation in which the work is experienced, and which demands the reader's participation. The book of course remains at the centre of such a situation, but the experience of the situation itself is controlled by the reader. His or her participation is not just the detached participation of an observer watching from a distance; it is a direct and active participation which involves even the reader's body, his or her movements. 'The proportions of the book are given by the proportions of the human hand', somebody once told me.

The ultimate book as a book preceded the golden era of artists' books by two centuries: it was published already in 1760. Laurence Sterne's *The Life and Opinions of Tristram Shandy, Gentleman* is a masterpiece of creative exploration of the semantic unity of all aspects of the book: its physical and material qualities, typography, the visual and textual content, the structure of the text. Sterne parodies the view of the tradition of the book as a history of a cumulative prolification of texts (in an almost postmodernist fashion). Towards the beginning of *Tristram Shandy*, Sterne asks: 'Tell me, ye learned reader, shall we for ever . . . make new books as apothecaries make mixtures, by pouring only out of one vesel into another?' Is it possible to make books which are anything other than re-formulations of knowledge contained in, and reflected by, the constantly growing body of literature?

The answer given by Sterne's book is neither yes nor no. It is difficult to conceive of books which would be entirely 'original' (in Sterne's terms, i.e. not merely different) because it is its ties with the tradition of books which make every book what it is. It seems to Sterne possible, however, even if only to prove a point, to make a book which will provoke a new kind of reading. Such a book would, of course, have to be self-defining as a book — that is to say, its being a book would have to be, in some way, synonymous with its contents.

Sterne makes a clear distinction between the 'story' and the 'book', and between 'telling', 'writing' and 'reading'. In Volume VI, Sterne demonstrates by graphic means that the twists and turns of the story do not parallel the linear progression of 'writing':

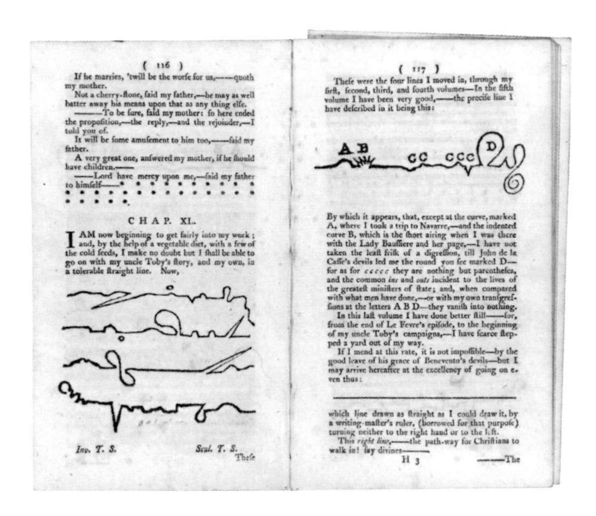

(116)

If he marries, 'twill be the worſe for us,——quoth my mother.

Not a cherry-ſtone, ſaid my father,—he may as well batter away his means upon that as any thing elſe.

———To be ſure, ſaid my mother: ſo here ended the propoſition,—the reply,—and the rejoinder,—I told you of.

It will be ſome amuſement to him too,——ſaid my father.

A very great one, anſwered my mother, if he ſhould have children.——

——Lord have mercy upon me,—ſaid my father to himſelf——* *.

CHAP. XL.

I AM now beginning to get fairly into my work; and, by the help of a vegetable diet, with a few of the cold ſeeds, I make no doubt but I ſhall be able to go on with my uncle Toby's ſtory, and my own, in a tolerable ſtraight line. Now,

Inv. T. S. Scul. T. S.

Theſe

(117)

Theſe were the four lines I moved in, through my firſt, ſecond, third, and fourth volumes—In the fifth volume I have been very good,——the preciſe line I have deſcribed in it being this:

By which it appears, that, except at the curve, marked A, where I took a trip to Navarre,—and the indented curve B, which is the ſhort airing when I was there with the Lady Bauſſiere and her page,—I have not taken the leaſt friſk of a digreſſion, till John de la Caſſe's devils led me the round you ſee marked D—for as for *c c c c c* they are nothing but parentheſes, and the common *ins* and *outs* incident to the lives of the greateſt miniſters of ſtate; and, when compared with what men have done,—or with my own tranſgreſſions at the letters A B D—they vaniſh into nothing.

In this laſt volume I have done better ſtill——for, from the end of Le Fevre's epiſode, to the beginning of my uncle Toby's campaigns,—I have ſcarce ſtepped a yard out of my way.

If I mend at this rate, it is not impoſſible—by the good leave of his grace of Benevento's devils—but I may arrive hereafter at the excellency of going on even thus:

which line drawn as ſtraight as I could draw it, by a writing-maſter's ruler, (borrowed for that purpoſe) turning neither to the right hand or to the left.

This *right line*,——the path-way for Chriſtians to walk in! ſay divines——

H 3 ——The

These were the four lines I moved in through my first, second, third, and fourth volumes

Elsewhere, a similar graphic device acknowledges the limits of the verbal language of story telling:

Whilst a man is free — cried the Corporal, giving a flourish with his stick thus —

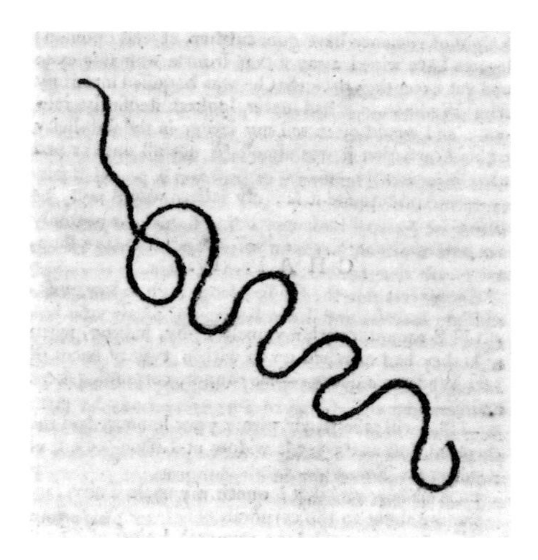

A thousand of my father's most subtle syllogisms could not have said more for celibacy

In Volume VII, a story within a story is not so much 'told' as distributed in space. Each attempt of the speaker (Corporal Trim) to resume telling the anecdote after having been interrupted by one of his audience is marked in the typography of the book by repeating the heading:

The story of the king of Bohemia
and his seven castes

The order of some chapters throughout the book is reversed, as if the reader should skip several pages and return to them later; chapters are reduced to a single line of text or omitted entirely. In one instance, the passage of time is suggested by the sentence,

My uncle Toby's Map is carried down to the kitchen

being placed in the middle of an otherwise blank page (as though the reader had to wait a little for the story to continue). The death of a village parson named Yorick (in a chapter alluding to Shakespeare and Cervantes) is symbolised by a page printed black, suggesting an ineffable content which cannot be 'read' in a conventional sense.

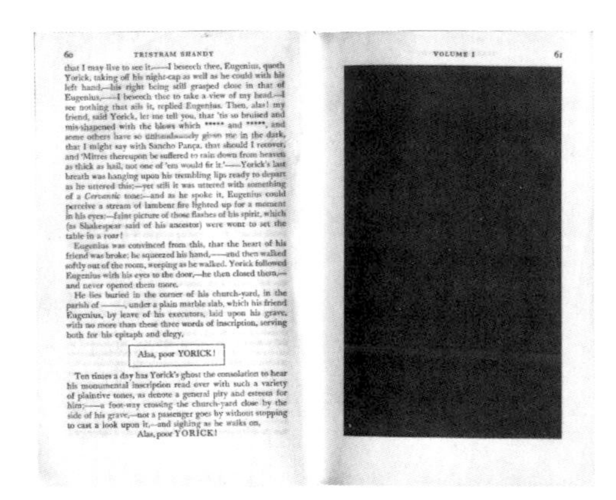
60 TRISTRAM SHANDY

that I may live to see it.——I beseech thee, Eugenius, quoth Yorick, taking off his night-cap as well as he could with his left hand,—his right being still grasped close in that of Eugenius,——I beseech thee to take a view of my head.—I see nothing that ails it, replied Eugenius. Then, alas! my friend, said Yorick, let me tell you, that 'tis so bruised and mis-shapened with the blows which ***** and *****, and some others have so unhandsomely given me in the dark, that I might say with Sancho Pança, that should I recover, and 'Mitres thereupon be suffered to rain down from heaven as thick as hail, not one of 'em would fit it.'——Yorick's last breath was hanging upon his trembling lips ready to depart as he uttered this;—yet still it was uttered with something of a *Cervantic* tone;—and as he spoke it, Eugenius could perceive a stream of lambent fire lighted up for a moment in his eyes;—faint picture of those flashes of his spirit, which (as Shakespear said of his ancestor) were wont to set the table in a roar!

Eugenius was convinced from this, that the heart of his friend was broke; he squeezed his hand,——and then walked softly out of the room, weeping as he walked. Yorick followed Eugenius with his eyes to the door,—he then closed them,—and never opened them more.

He lies buried in the corner of his church-yard, in the parish of ——, under a plain marble slab, which his friend Eugenius, by leave of his executors, laid upon his grave, with no more than these three words of inscription, serving both for his epitaph and elegy.

Alas, poor YORICK!

Ten times a day has Yorick's ghost the consolation to hear his monumental inscription read over with such a variety of plaintive tones, as denote a general pity and esteem for him;——a foot-way crossing the church-yard close by the side of his grave,—not a passenger goes by without stopping to cast a look upon it,—and sighing as he walks on,

Alas, poor YORICK!

VOLUME I 61

Yet, the reader is prompted to 'read' an equally illegible marbled page later on in the book:

Read, read, read, read, my unlearned reader! — or by the knowledge of the great saint *Paraleipomenon* — I tell you before-hand, you had better throw down the book at once; for without *much reading*, by which your reverence knows, I mean *much knowledge*, you will no more be able to penetrate the moral of the next marbled page (motly emblem of my work!) than the world with all its sagacity has been able to unraval the many opinions, transactions and truths which still lie mystically hid under the dark veil of the black one.

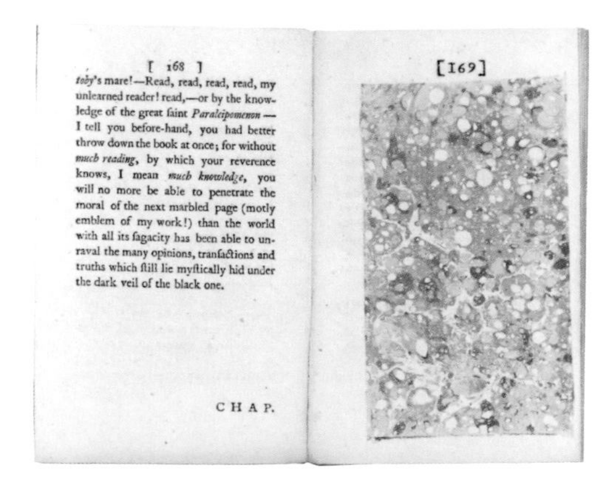
[168]

toby's mare!—Read, read, read, read, my unlearned reader! read,—or by the knowledge of the great ſaint *Paraleipomenon* — I tell you before-hand, you had better throw down the book at once; for without *much reading*, by which your reverence knows, I mean *much knowledge*, you will no more be able to penetrate the moral of the next marbled page (motly emblem of my work!) than the world with all its ſagacity has been able to unraval the many opinions, tranſactions and truths which ſtill lie myſtically hid under the dark veil of the black one.

CHAP.

[169]

There are also some odd blank pages in *Tristram Shandy*: two for the chapters left out, and another one for the reader to describe in his or her own words the beauty of one Widow Wadman. These blank pages reflect two different aspects of the relationship between the book and the reader. The empty space of the missing chapters points towards the physicality of the book. The textual information, save the chapter headings, has been withdrawn by the author. The reader is presented with two blank pages which interrupt the flow of the story and which literally obstruct the progress through the text. There is nothing to read and yet the pages have to be turned over ('read') in precisely the same way as other pages for the story to continue.[5] Confronted with the 'book as book', the reader is reminded that reading a book always also demands considering its real space.

The emptiness of the third page is very different. It identifies the book as the borderline between the physical and the spiritual worlds. It is the emptiness of an empty frame, it invites the reader to participate spiritually in the substance of the book. It doesn't obstruct, it opens the way by which to enter the metaphorical 'space' of the story. But even this spiritual space is contained within the physical space of the book; it is *inside* the book.

It is through the quality of having an inside that another kind of relationship between books and people is, at least symbolically, established. It has been said that everything in the world exists only to end up in books, that our lives, history and knowledge are *contained* in and by books. Books are both a part and a product of human history and civilization, and the guardians and the protagonists of its continuity. They take their part in the world through their interaction with people — influencing and changing our perception of the world . . . which in turn might become the contents of future books.

The participatory nature of the relationship between people and the book, and its anthropomorphic quality of having an inside, or inner life (and so being capable of self-reflection) makes the book the frame for the understanding and expression of the world, of which the book is an integral part, and for which it is a most potent metaphor.

It seems that the self-reflective capacity of the book to hold its own history and its substance within itself, makes it possible for the book to be a work of art (or a part of such) whilst retaining its identity as a book and its links with the world outside art (the world of everyday books). The book in art is always also a 'space' in which the qualities of the book, its tradition, history, the continuity of its development, and all its symbolism can be encountered. Or, in other words, even in art books are just books.

1. *Books as Books*. Edited notes for a lecture given at Glasgow School of Art in November 1993, based in part on a catalogue essay for *Turning Over the Pages: Some Books in Contemporary Art* (Cambridge: Kettle's Yard, 1986).

2. Lucy R. Lippard, 'Conspicuous Consumption: New Artists' Books', *Artists' Books: A Critical Anthology and Sourcebook*, edited by Joan Lyons (Rochester: Visual Studies Workshop Press, 1985).

3. Ulises Carrión, Other Books & So stationery, Amsterdam, early 1970s; Hubert Kretchmer, 'Künstlerbücher? Objektbücher? Buchobjekte?', *Buchobjekte, Kunstlerbücher*, exhibition catalogue, Darmstadt, 1982; Paul-Armand Gette, 'Objekt-Buch-Objekt', *Akzente* 6, December 1979; Clive Phillpot, 'Book Art Digressions', *Artists' Books*, exhibition catalogue, Arts Council of Great Britain, London 1976 — later Phillpot added a further category of 'artists' booklets', in Printed Matter Catalog 1986/87, New York 1986; *Livres d'artistes*, curated by Anne Mœglin-Delcroix, Centre Georges Pompidou, Paris, 1985.

4. Ulises Carrión, 'The New Art of Making Books', *Kontexts* 6, Amsterdam, 1985.

5. The interest in what lies ahead has been often exploited in the opposite way in artists' books; through cutting holes in pages or printing on tracing paper, transparent plastic, etc.

6. Pages from *Tristram Shandy* are taken from early editions held in The British Library (shelf-marks 1613.bb.10 C.70.aa.28) and reproduced with permission, and from the Penguin edition.

ME AND ARTISTS' BOOKS
ANN GALLAGHER

All our incoming mail at the British Council Visual Arts Department is opened, referenced and sorted by a central Arts Division Registry. That is all mail not marked 'personal'. Personal mail is required to be opened in front of a member of Registry Department, 'just in case of cheques'. I presume what is meant is that in the unlikely event of someone sending a cheque to me at work, I would have to prove I was the rightful recipient or risk having said cheque confiscated.

In any case a package not marked 'personal' recently occasioned a curious member of Registry Department to call my extension and ask if I could spare the time to explain who Imprint 93 was and what the 'art' was that they appeared to have sent me. I suspected there may have been a degree of amusement lurking behind that request but the curiosity remained genuine. I was also impressed by the unhesitating use of the term 'art', for what I suspected may not have been immediately recognisable as such to just anybody.

Imprint 93 is the name of a potentially unlimited series of books/artworks published by Matthew Higgs and mailed at regular intervals to interested parties. I first became aware of the series when they began to appear in the post at Anthony Reynolds Gallery where I previously worked as a director (no Registry Department, in my day anyway). Each publication is made by a different artist, some more familiar to me than others, but slowly and almost in spite of myself I began to be intrigued by them.[1]

I say in spite of myself, because these could be described as 'artists' books' and I had decided a few years back to put a deal of distance between myself and artists' books. You see I used to be quite obsessed by them. Working in Nigel Greenwood Gallery in the mid-eighties I learned about conceptual art through the medium of artists' books. As larger and larger paintings were being sold in the eighties boom, I sat in basements (in Sloane Gardens and then in NG's new space in New Burlington Street) fascinated by a time that had just passed me by. I devoured all the text books and catalogues of the seminal shows. And learned the definition of an 'artist's

A sheet of A4 paper torn up

Martin Creed

Work No. 140 (43)

M Creed 1995

Imprint 93

book' as opposed to a *livre d'artiste* or a mere catalogue or magazine. I actually rather liked catalogues and magazines too (and still do).

As an offshoot of the main gallery we sold the latest international catalogues and books and made exhibitions of artists' books (Ian Hamilton Finlay, Dieter Roth), eventually extending to include objects and works on paper (John Baldessari, Barbara Kruger, David Tremlett), videos (Bruce Nauman, Nam June Paik), installations and performances (Stephen Willats, Silvia Ziranek). Initially we dealt in and showed work by artists who had been associated with the gallery over the years or artists who worked predominantly in the medium of books (Gilbert and George, Richard Long, Ed Ruscha) and gradually introduced a number of younger artists and publishers such as Jake Tilson, Parkett Magazine and the newly formed Paragon Press. It was exciting and fun and there was a dedicated audience out there.

But as the eighties progressed I am not sure if it was me who began to feel jaded or if the world of books had begun to resemble the art market it paralleled. Lavish publications began to appear for no particular reason. Every artist in the world seemed to have taken to 'the book form' and not all of them were particularly good at it. Things had to change. The whole area of publishing had to go through a major rethink. This was a time when the art magazine Artscribe went glossy and then died, while a new one called frieze (new, cheaper technology, simple design) had appeared and was gathering cult status. Maybe if I had hung around long enough I would have witnessed a gradual change, but I was restless.

Newly installed in another basement (Anthony Reynolds Gallery) you could hardly tell I had ever been an 'artist's book person' except for the occasional hint of an obsession with multiples. We put together a show of multiples including works by Nayland Blake, Marinus Boezum, Katherina Fritsch, Rebecca Horn, Pieter Laurens Mol, Lucia Nogueira, Jon Thompson, Jean-Luc Vilmouth and Lawrence Weiner. Then we helped Georgina Starr make an edition with a tape and a sort of book in it, and I was getting excited again. I was beginning to be cured of my anathema.

Opposite: *Work No. 140.* A sheet of A4 paper torn up. Martin Creed, Imprint 93 (1995)

With the benefit of hindsight it now seems clearer to me that it remains a fascinating area just so long as the artists involved are making the sort of work that demands to be made in this form. I have a great deal of respect for the stayers in the field, artists who have consistently chosen to make books and just plain can't stop. I also admire the publishers who have managed to evolve with the times, those with a keen eye for the sort of artists who are able to see making books as a natural extension of their own work and not because it is a cute thing to do or as an alternative to knitting. (Those such as Coracle and its outlet and lively exhibition programme workfortheeyetodo; Book Works, whose recent backlist reads like a pretty impressive exhibition programme; Jack Wendler in his joint venture with Liam Gillick, G+W Press). A lot of younger artists working today, said to be influenced by the conceptual art practice of the seventies, have turned out the odd book, unselfconsciously and when the form was appropriate, and there is a re-emergence of interesting work.

So back to the Registry Room. It was Imprint, *Work No. 140. A sheet of A4 paper torn up* by Martin Creed. I was proud of the British Council Arts Division Registry Department. Not a single piece was missing. It could easily have been one of those 'the cleaner who swept away half a Richard Long piece' stories. And my friend there listened to my description of other work by the artist, other artists' works for the series and I hope got something out of it. Maybe it truly is an accessible artform.

1. Imprint 93 has so far comprised works by: Fiona Banner, Paul Bloodgood, Pavel Büchler, Cabinet Gallery, Billy Childish, City Racing, Matthew Collings, Martin Creed, Neil Cummings, Jeremy Deller, Peter Doig, Ceal Floyer, Matthew Higgs, Stewart Home, Alan Kane, Liebscher-Lehanka, Hilary Lloyd, Colin Lowe, Jeff Luke, Thomas Nicolaou, Paul Noble, Simon Periton, Elizabeth Peyton, James Pyman, Maggie Roberts, Bob and Roberta Smith, Roddy Thompson, Jessica Voorsanger, Christopher Warmington, Stephen Willats, Elizabeth Wright.

Book Works, London Bridge (1984)

Book Works began its existence in three railway arches in Borough Market at London Bridge in 1984, which were rented from the British Rail Property Board. Twelve years later it now occupies a newly converted building near Liverpool Street Station. When Book Works first began, it was set up in an attempt to position the book in terms of contemporary art practice and to give it a relevant context; this remains a constant concern today, despite the organisational development and the changes of structure. In fact it is Book Works' ability to change, to continually examine what it is trying to achieve, that has made it an exciting place to work.

The group that originally started Book Works had many discussions about what it was we wanted to do. We were all practising as freelance printers, printmakers and book-binders, but felt isolated, part of some craft 'backwater' and wanted a space where we could show new work, organise events, collaborate with others and generate an interest and context for our own work. The early days at Book Works were a struggle; we worked mainly on a voluntary basis, initially with the help of a small setting-up grant from the Crafts Council. There was however a wide support group and growing interest in what we were trying to do that kept us going. We organised a series of exhibitions and events in a gallery space we converted in the railway arches, and the plan was to show mainly new work by contemporary artists using the book form.

Crisis of Western Education
Langlands and Bell (1984)
Sculpture, with books and objects
Ruth & Marvin Sackner Collection

Artists like Langlands and Bell were exploring the iconic and sculptural properties of the book through their early work, as seen in their exhibition at Book Works, *The Ruined Book* (1984), whilst Art in Ruins (Hannah Vowles, Glyn Banks and John Coleman) used the book as part of a larger installation, *Work From the Ruins* (1985), part of their strategy of questioning the institutions of art and culture itself. Pavel Büchler's publication and installation, *The Wall: 2200th Anniversary of the Great Wall of China, Berlin 1961-86*, was a similar attempt to position the book in the context of an installation, that asked its viewers to make connections at some distance from where they stood. Other shows included work by artists and publishers who were already well established including Ian Tyson, Ron King and Circle Press, Dieter Rot, editions hansjörg mayer, Ken Campbell, and relative newcomers like Susan Johanknecht, Liver and Lights, the Oblivion Boys, David Sellars, Jake Tilson, and Hangman Press (amongst others) in a variety of solo, group and theme shows.

Work from Common Knowledge
Glyn Banks, John Coleman, Hannah Vowles, published by Circle Press (1985)

The Wall: 2200th Anniversary of the Great Wall of China, Berlin 1961-1986 installation by Pavel Büchler (1986)

During this time we also organised two projects, *Site Works I* (1986) and *Site Works II* (1988) which took place in and around Borough Market, as a result of an open submission for proposals by artists to produce site-specific works. The artists that were commissioned included Richard Layzell, Cornelia Parker, Langlands & Bell, Stefan Szczelkun, Jo Stockham and Brian Catling. These two projects marked the beginnings of organising events and exhibitions that took place in different sites. While this grew out of a desire to work within our immediate neighbourhood, a part of London with a rich history in a period of development and rapid change, the preoccupation with site and location was shared with many artists and we have continued to develop it by commissioning and working with artists using various media.

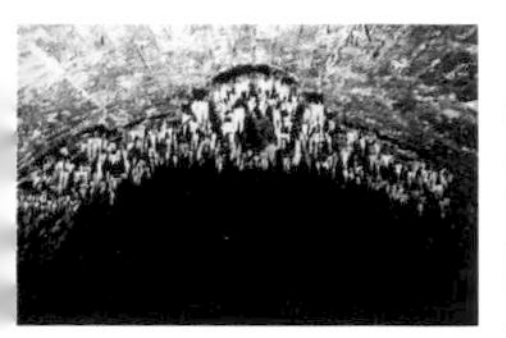

Stalactite City
Cornelia Parker
Site Works I (1986)
Hundreds of tiny lead cathedrals, installation outside Book Works, London Bridge

After about three years we took a decision to close the gallery space, partly as we were finding it a financial struggle, but also in response to a general feeling that we would rather concentrate our energies on commissioning artists to publish and make work in collaboration with Book Works, and to curate exhibitions for other venues allowing us more scope. Although Book Works has always relied partly on grants to help subsidise the programme of activities, and now receives support from the Arts Council of England, the London Arts Board and other sponsors, we have always retained a separate commercial side to the organisation through the studio which undertakes a wide variety of commissioned work.

Something should also be said here about the individuals that go to make up Book Works. We have remained a small group bringing in other people with specific skills and experience when needed. Of the original group of five who started Book Works, Rob Hadrill and Jane Rolo remain as working directors. Although all policy and financial decisions are taken together for both sides of the business, on a daily basis Rob Hadrill runs the studio and all commissioned works, working with a team of four or five printers and bookbinders, whilst Jane Rolo is in charge of the publishing and projects programme, together with Anna Pank who handles Book Works' development, marketing and distribution. In addition to this, extra freelance help (designers, editors, photographers) is recruited to contribute to the publications and to help with research, technical, and curatorial assistance on the projects. Because of our size and the overlap between the kinds of work we publish and which is passing through the studio, final design decisions (always the most difficult part of publishing) usually involve everyone.

Book Works has been publishing artists' books since 1987, and has established itself as a leading independent publisher over recent years. Invited artists are commissioned to collaborate with Book Works, and proposals are also considered through a programme of open submission. Rather than focusing on the more illustrative tradition of the *livre d'artiste* or craft-orientated bookmaking, Book Works commissions interdisciplinary projects with artists which are more closely related to contemporary visual arts, especially to conceptual, installation and performance work.

Unlike many publishers, Book Works likes to collaborate with the artists from the start of each book, rather than responding to a 'ready-made' proposal, acting as commissioning agent as well as publisher. So although we collaborate with artists who have firm ideas about the presentation of their work, which the diversity of the appearance of the books demonstrates, the final appearance is rarely predictable in advance. It is perhaps one of the reasons that we produce relatively few titles in a year, as the work is often involved and complicated, and not suitable for a conveyor-belt form of publishing.

The starting point for each book is the content, whether this is the artist's response to a theme Book Works has suggested (as with the open submission proposals) or part of a larger body of work that the artist may be working on, that is to find a different context and meanings within the book form. The physical character of the book, in terms of dimensions, choice of materials and design, sequence of pages, and the relation of text and image are important to establish. These factors will transform and in a sense function as the subject-matter of the book; and though the final effect of the combination of materials is never quite predictable, even when the decisions have been made, we try to envisage the relationship the book will establish with the reader as fully as possible.

Places to Remember
Lily R. Markiewicz
installation to accompany publication of *The Price of Words*, *Book Works: A Women's Perspective* (1992)

The book often allows an artist to explore their ideas within a new context, and we must be certain that the format is the right one to follow with each book that is published, determining a strong work which can stand on its own. The first books published, *Very Food* by Silvia Ziranek, *Guidelines to the System* by Verdi Yahooda, *Notable Days* by Pavel Büchler, *The Stumbling Block, its Index* by Brian Catling, *The Price of Words* by Lily R. Markiewicz and *Reading the Glass: Management of the Eyes, Moderation of the Gaze* by Sharon Kivland, Charles Barber and Conrad Leyser — all these books were presented within the context of an exhibition, performance, conference or time-based work to help locate them within a framework of visual arts practice and more simply as a way of promoting and selling them. Recently the books have come to stand more on their own, perhaps with a launch event staged in a more conventional way, although several books have been developed as a parallel work to installations and events that we have commissioned — *Two Oxford Reading Rooms* by Joseph Kosuth, *The Blindings* by Brian Catling and *After the Freud Museum* by Susan Hiller.

Edition numbers for the books are usually between 500 and 1,000 copies, and in some cases a special limited edition is also published, usually produced at Book Works. Limited editions are also made with some artists where larger editions would not be suitable (usually because they are printed and bound by hand), for example the books produced with Chris Newman, *Supplement* by Avis Newman, or the multiple *Left Over (Residue)* by Susan Hiller. As well as individual titles published at Book Works, we have established two continuing

series for our list which engage slightly differently with the traditions of artists' books and show our interest in forming alliances beyond contemporary art.

The Format Series. The idea behind this series was to make artists' books that were accessible, cheap and desirable, using a small, pocket-sized format. The series so far includes *Rex Reason* by Simon Patterson and *Two Oxford Reading Rooms* by Joseph Kosuth. The next two titles will be a book by Douglas Gordon and one by Paul Etienne Lincoln, the English artist living in New York known for his engineering and inventiveness.

The New Writing Series has evolved out of a desire to publish work that crosses the boundary between art and literature, making a distinct niche for writing by artists, and by writers with a questioning attitude towards form or who are curious about the connections their interests may have with visual art and its audience. Michael Bracewell is guest editor for the series, which has been selected from an open submission for proposals. The first two books in the series are *Err* by David Shrigley and *Confessions* by Jeremy Millar, and a third book by Deborah Levy has been commissioned.

In addition to the books and multiples we have also published two videotapes, *J'appelle un chat un chat* by Shelagh Wakely and *Scroll* by Brian Catling (co-published with The British Library). We are also co-publishing our first CD-Rom, *Rehearsal of Memory* by Harwood (with Artec in association with Ashworth Arts). Although this represents a move to a new technology, the subject-matter, derived from Graham Harwood's work with patients and staff at Ashworth, a high-security hospital, is disturbing, and protests against many of the associations new technology inevitably has. The possibilities the CD-Rom form offer for

Opposite: *Me.* Chris Newman, detail fom book published by Book Works (1993)

interactivity are used to bring the reader/user close up to aspects of the lives of mentally ill individuals, while also questioning what kind of 'contact' is possible through technological means alone. As such, the commissioning of the CD-Rom builds on Book Works' philosophy — a questioning attitude to all that is involved in 'reading' — and takes it into a new stage.

No longer having a dedicated exhibition space, we have been able to show work since 1987 in very different kinds of venues, freeing us also to do some larger scale projects. Over the years we have been attracted to working in very different kinds of spaces, from pristine galleries to old buildings, indoor and outdoor sites, and of course libraries, from the large national collections to the smaller libraries that remain such important and well-used resources.

The book is such a familiar object to us all, and yet may soon become a relic, a curious object from the past, to be found, stored and catalogued in specialist libraries. *Collected Works* aims to present work that perhaps defies simple categorisation, and looks at the relationship between printed matter, libraries and the people that use them.
Collected Works leaflet text, 1993

Time Piece. Gary Stevens, live art event for *Collected Works* at the National Art Library, Victoria & Albert Museum (1993)

Libraries are never empty 'white' anonymous spaces where a spectator can interact with an art work in an uninterrupted way, but have different resonances, histories and specific functions that continually crowd the picture, both physically and conceptually, making references between the artists' work and the space necessary. Projects that have involved working closely with libraries have included *Collected Works* (1993) which presented a series of new commissions in five libraries in the Royal Borough of Kensington and Chelsea, including the National Art Library at the Victoria and Albert Museum; and *The Reading Room* (1994), which included works made for The British Library, London, the Voltaire Library, Taylor Institute and the Bodleian Library, Oxford. We are currently commissioning a series of new works for the University of London Library (Senate House); the British Architectural Library at RIBA, London; the Central Library, Liverpool; and Chetham's Library, Manchester, as part of a project called *Library Re-Locations*, which extends some of the ideas inherent in *The Reading Room* project by inviting artists to act as researchers in four libraries with special collections, and to make works for their particular environments.

L'attente......L'oubli installation by Sharon Kivland *Book Works: A Women's Perspective* (1992)

Most of the projects that we initiate have a connecting theme to the work that we commission. One of the first large projects we organised was called *Book Works: A Women's Perspective* in 1992, which was an attempt to look at women's involvement in all aspects of book production, as artists, writers, critics, and curators. We included an exhibition of artists' books by women, two new installations, a two day conference, with performances and the launch of two books.

Itinerant Texts (1996) is a multiple using slide works commissioned as part of the travelling exhibition *Artist/Author: The Book As Art Since 1980.* It includes some artists we have worked with and some with whom we are less familiar, from different countries[1]. By using a miniature format, the multiple functions as a portable exhibition or anthology of work that can be shown anywhere there is a screen and a projector. As such it extends the debate about site-specificity and 'art beyond the gallery', by attempting to come up with a form that is the opposite of site-specific, and which has a kind of modesty. It captures something of the hectic circumstances in which many artists now work, flying from place to place in order to 'respond' to locations where they are to make or show work, and sometimes wondering what their audience are getting out of it. As Jimmie Durham puts it:

> These days I am travelling around the continent of Eurasia as much as possible but always the first impression of any place (or any person) is incomprehension and then the feeling that the incomprehension is intrinsic; that I will never understand anything . . .

The following is taken from an original essay by Jane Rolo for *Artist/Author: The Book As Art Since 1980* by Cornelia Lauf and Clive Phillpot, to be published by the American Federation of Arts and Distributed Art Publishers, New York, in 1997):

When I was thinking of ideas for Book Works' contribution to *Artist/Author* a couple of years ago, I became interested in the nature of the artist continually working a kind of circuit. It seemed to me I suddenly knew a lot of artists who were on the move, responding to the next project or installation, travelling from place to place, making work for different spaces. Nothing particularly new in this but I wondered how it might affect an artist's way of working. I thought it could be interesting to use this as the starting point for a project, to comment on the shifts within an artist's own work in response to this movement, and how they tackled making a work for the next venue or site-specific location.

The nature of this show, being planned to tour to unknown venues, meant I wanted to come up with a versatile solution and to commission work that really would travel. So I decided that the work should be made in the form of a series of slides or *itinerant texts* to be projected directly onto the wall in each location. I liked the idea of a portable work, that could be unpacked, and viewed like holiday snap-shots, transporting the viewer to different corners of the world either literally or conceptually. My job as a curator and an editor would be to shape and order the work, like putting together a journal or magazine of various contributions. The difference between producing a book and creating an installation like this became more to do with scale and versatility, with the projected images forming a progression of time-based works, like turning the pages of a book.

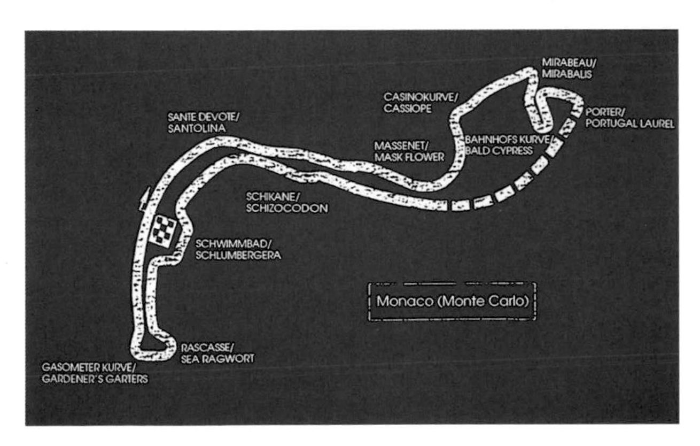

Untitled. Simon Patterson, part of *Itinerant Texts* installation and multiple of slide works (1996)

Artists all bring their different styles to a project like this, being influenced by different approaches to their work and responding to the theme in a variety of ways. The projected images produced by the artists all contain texts, generated using different media from hand-written texts to computer-generated images; the subject matter is often self-referential, commenting on the artist's own position as an *itinerant*, or may refer to other projects that are being worked on.

The invited artists live in cities in Europe and the USA, but constantly seemed to be displaced, travelling to another country or continent. The communications between the artists and myself by letter, fax and telephone speak for themselves about how much travelling is involved. Endless *itineraries* from the artists about where they would be, when, and for how long made me ponder on their lives and how their work must change or adapt to suit this type of existence, compared with my own fairly fixed one.

My role as editor and curator means that I have laid down my own reading of the images to form a kind of narrative from all the material, the artists leaving this decision and responsibility to me. I hope I have done their collective works justice, and that in the viewer's reading, the sentiments of Douglas Gordon's piece might be echoed: *'I've changed. You've changed.'*

1. Judith Barry, Robert Barry, Angela Bulloch, Tacita Dean, Jimmie Durham, Tracey Emin, Liam Gillick, Douglas Gordon, Susan Hiller, Joseph Kosuth, Tracy Mackenna and Simon Patterson.

This project brought together many of the different aspects that go to make up Book Works and the energy and creativity that were generated by the artists and other contributors has continued well after the event.

Above: *Say: I Do Not Know.* Joseph Kosuth, installation at the Divinity School, Bodleian Library, Oxford
Opposite: detail of texts screen-printed on wooden freestanding signs

The Reading Room (1994) took the form of a series of new commissions by artists and writers on the theme of books, reading and knowledge. Book Works invited those participating to create their own versions of a reading room both as physical sites and conceptual spaces in which dialogues might take place, and for them to highlight, through the use of the physical settings or the contrast with them, something of the complexity of the ways in which we make our various paths to knowledge.

The Reading Room aimed to pose questions about the relationship between text and image in culture and in art practice today, looking at how we 'read' art, and at what the future may bring in terms of expanding our experience of reading. Specifically the project and its settings encouraged speculation on the relationships between how, and where and why information and knowledge is received, stored and valued. Implicitly, the theme suggested an examination of the gaps and blind spots in our knowledge, but auto-biographical accounts of how people read what they did were inevitable, and provided a less tense atmosphere in which to think about these questions. The artists and writers responded by creating imagined reading rooms about which and in which these debates might take place.

Previous page: *Scroll.* Brian Catling, performance at The British Library

part(?)
Amongst such kind of collective *Ideas*, are to be counted most part of artificial Things, at least such of them as are made up of distinct Substances: and, in truth, if we consider all these collective *Ideas* aright, as *ARMY, Constellation, Universe*; as they are united into so many single *Ideas*, they are but the artificial Draughts of the Mind, bringing things very remote, and independent on one another, into one view, the better to contemplate, and discourse of them, united into one conception, and signified by one name.
The owl, who feeds on mice in his shanty, said to the nightingale: 'Stop singing in your shady trees, come into my hole for me to devour you'; and the nightingale replied: 'I was born to sing here and to laugh at you.'
You ask me what will become of freewill. I don't understand you. I do not know what this freewill is that you speak of. You have been arguing for so long about its nature that you assuredly do not know.

The reading rooms were made in a variety of different locations in London, Glasgow and Oxford, including regular exhibition spaces such as Camden Arts Centre in London, Museum of Modern Art, Oxford and Transmission Gallery in Glasgow. In all of these galleries the writers (Michael Bracewell, Jackie Kay, Janice Galloway) interpreted their notion of a reading room in a visual setting. Libraries and museum spaces like the Bodleian Library and Voltaire Room, Oxford, The British Library and the Freud Museum in London provided sites for work that was determined by association and by the nature of the space itself, whilst places like the Castle Mound, Oxford and the Royal Botanic Garden in Edinburgh had a particular resonance as places where temporary, alternative reading rooms could be imagined as against those that actually exist.

The (Ethical) Space of Cabinets 7 & 8. Joseph Kosuth,
installation at the Voltaire Room, Taylor Institution, Oxford University, now permanently installed

The project was co-curated by Susan Brind and Jane Rolo, and involved a huge amount of organisation and planning with the many different organisations and individuals involved. In addition to the commissioned works, there were other events including a programme of artists' videos curated by Breda Beban and Hrvoje Horvatic, artists working in video in ways that visually parallel the techniques and effects of poetry; a lecture by Sean Cubitt, *Cyber Books Read Only Memories* on the impact of new technologies on reading; readings by the three writers we had persuaded to present their thoughts in galleries, and a symposium in Glasgow at which some of the many debates possible were had; and not least an exhibition, *Reading the Book*, which toured to

Opposite: detail from *The (Ethical) Space of Cabinets 7 & 8*

Rousseau
Rousseau
Rousseau
VOLTAIRE ROOM CUPBOARDS
CONTENTS
In some of our *Ideas* there are certain Relations, Habitudes, and Connexions, so visibly included in the Nature of the *Ideas* themselves, that we cannot conceive them separable from them, by any Power whatsoever. And in these only, we are capable of certain and universal Knowledge.
The dwarf, who sometimes judged
a little too hastily, decided at once
that there was no one on the earth,
his first reason being that he had seen
no one. Micromegas politely made
him feel that it was a poor enough
reason. 'With your little eyes,' he
said, 'you do not see certain stars
of the fiftieth magnitude which I
perceive very distinctly. Do you
these stars do not exist?'
5. Microfilm of the St. Petersburg copy of the 1775 edition of Voltaire's works [annotated by him], 21 boxes [administrative papers], duplicates of various books, tapes, slides and records of Voltaire works

local libraries and was intended to re-address some of the questions involved for those less familiar with or interested in going to art exhibitions or events.

The project allowed Book Works the opportunity and scope to collaborate with both artists and writers on exciting and difficult new work, and subsequently three important artists' books were published in parallel to works commissioned for *The Reading Room*. The books (*Two Oxford Reading Rooms* by Joseph Kosuth, *After the Freud Museum* by Susan Hiller and *The Blindings* by Brian Catling) allow a more permanent reading and re-capitulation of some of the original work, and are considered elsewhere in this book. The space given to recording the project here indicates the wide range of ways in which the artists and writers have responded to the theme, the way it has provoked reflection at an autobiographical as well as a more conceptual, removed standpoint.

Opposite: *Susan Hiller at the Freud Museum*. Detail of one of boxes from installation at the Freud Museum, London, *Virgula Divina/water witching. Displayed, 1991*

photocopy of artist's notes on dowsing methods; artist's hand-made divining rods; two pendulae, one hand-made in customized cardboard box, labelled (33 x 25.5 x 6.5 cm)

Susan Hiller describes this box in her book, *After the Freud Museum*: 'I made the divining rods and pendulum when I was learning to dowse. The process of dowsing is very systematic, although no one can explain why it works when it works. The notes give a few procedures and formulas, mainly derived from the work of Lethbridge, a respected British archaeologist.'

make 2 angle rods
& 1 pendulum:

Long pendulum for
walking in field
but short for
map work

get a brass
plumb for the
long pend. - must
be heavy

Dowsing rod—
"Bishops Rule"

BENEATH THE SURFACE

MICHAEL BRACEWELL

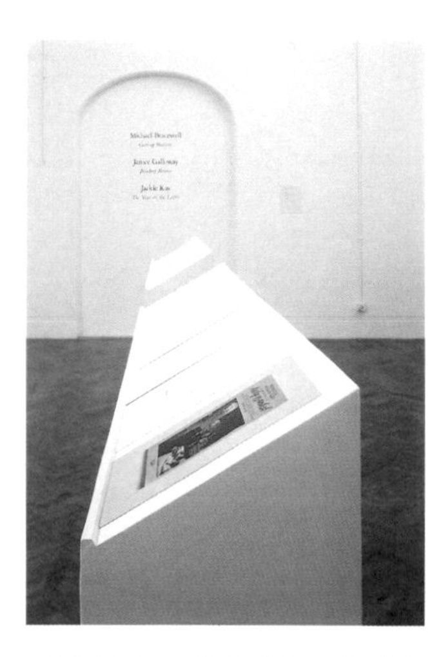

Writers' Reading Room. Michael Bracewell, Jackie Kay and Janice Galloway, installation at Camden Arts Centre, London. Detail of *Getting Shallow* by Michael Bracewell. Slanting shelf with text and image panels

The relationship between literature and the visual arts has always been more of an affair than a marriage. It has been far more common, in cultural history, to find artists who wrote as opposed to writers who made art, and the literary artists tend to be individuals who are driven by a particular philosophy — usually a philosophy of protest or warning. One can take a line — from William Blake as a rebel romantic, to the ease in both media of Wyndham Lewis, Cecil Collins and, more recently, the late Derek Jarman. Added to this could be the mystical fiction written by Leonora Carrington, with its rehearsal of magic realism, and — at the other end of the literary scale — the opaque writings of Gilbert and George with their somewhat Maoist sense of 'Little Red Book' style Collected Thoughts. With the exception of Carrington, for whom literature was a further retreat into the fabulism of her autobiographical paintings, all of these literary artists can be seen as working traditionally in separate media, writing journals, fiction or philosophical pensées as a complement to, but independent of, their 'day jobs' as primarily visual artists. There is no real sense in which their writings should be considered as visual statements per se.

With Fluxus and conceptualism, much of this separation between the literary and the visual began to change; texts — whether instruction paintings, displayed statements or even lists — could be seen as both visual and literary, requiring the viewers to break down their traditional expectations. Text, for visual artists, could be used as a medium in its own right, and the book form (as one can see from the body of work assembled by Book Works) could function either by aspiring to the traditional high aesthetics of the 'artist's book', or as a less crafted but equally effective means of extending a visual project. Now, with the introduction of information technology to the media of visual art, the boundaries between fine art and literature have become even more blurred, to the point of making any critical distinction between them in those terms much harder to justify. *The Reading Room*, as an investigation by writers and artists into the important subject of books and reading, on both a personal and archival level, demanded an over-view of the relationship between literary and visual art, from the role of text within art to the constitution of libraries and bibliographical information as both metaphor and reality. The Reading Room, as a common theme, served both as a subject for autobiographical reflection and for conceptual interpretation.

One of the most interesting results of *The Reading Room* project was the discovery that while visual art has actively sought an experimental relationship with literature, rehearsed by the conceptualism of the last thirty years, the world of literature has remained largely unresponsive to that dialogue. In the affair between words and pictures, literature has been a somewhat stroppy partner. And, in some ways, one can see why. Literature, for most writers, is a closed practice which answers only to its own traditional rules — however touched by the avant garde in terms of technique and subject. As E.M. Forster remarked back in 1922, in his *Aspects of the Novel*, 'The novel, oh dear yes, the novel tells a story', and telling stories, be they ever so fractured or self-reflective, remains central to effective literature. With the reading room, however, as a theme to be explored by writers and artists, it was important and timely that both camps should analyse the dynamics of their relationship to one another, asking certain questions of themselves that were necessarily more personal than theoretical. Indeed, as critical theory has developed over the last twenty years to be a kind of cultural esperanto, capable of deconstructing anything within range, *The Reading Room* offered a rare meeting between literature and visual art away from what has become a critical No-Man's Land. Writers and artists were presenting their work on its own terms, with no concessions to the levelling terminology that can turn cultural debate into a mere exchange of opinions. As such, *The Reading Room* could be seen as a modernist as opposed to a postmodern project, stringently traditional despite the radicalism of its intention.

For a writer, the challenge to present an interpretation of the reading room in a way that was both visual and literary (the venue for the project being within a gallery rather than between hard covers) was to usefully force an exercise in conceptual thinking. Inevitably, the subject raised personal speculation on the relationship between creativity and the role of the archive. The question raised was Sartre's chilling demand of writers: 'For whom are you writing?' As a novelist, my interest has always been in a form of naturalism that is closer to documentary, in terms of both style and content, than it is to poetics or experiments with style. I try to find my stories in the mundane, and the extraordinary seems most present in the unremittingly ordinary. Extreme states of mind and extreme states of behaviour always seem closer to the usual than the unusual. Hence my choice of Warhol and Flaubert as twin patron saints of my Reading Room, considered as a literary and personal shrine. It seemed largely immaterial that Warhol is seen as an artist and Flaubert as a writer; their mutual project was a desire to reflect the world exactly as they found it, neither judging nor romanticising but allowing description to stand for itself. Between them, they seemed to cover the human condition as both tragedy and comedy, presenting near mimesis as the portal to complex statements about how we live in society. Similarly, they both bridged romanticism and realism, describing the intimate relationship between those seemingly opposed positions; the young Flaubert who wrote *The Temptation of Saint Anthony* was as dedicated to the demands of craft as the young Warhol who designed shoes for rich Fifth Avenue ladies.

In the presentation of my essay for *The Reading Room*, as a personal appraisal of Warhol and Flaubert (usefully, Warhol sub-contracted his literary project to Bob Colacello and Pat Hackett, who transcribed his thoughts into a literary form which is suprisingly close to the naturalistic novel) it seemed vital that a Flaubertian text should be displayed in a Warholian manner, with the minimum of clutter, adorment or self-conscious style. Warhol, I felt would have said, 'Oh, it would be great to just put the pages in the gallery', while Flaubert, disdaining any deviation from the purity of literature, would have demanded a similar simplicity within the text. *The Reading Room*, for me, was a reminder that simplicity is the hardest thing of all. Hence the title of my piece, *Getting Shallow*.[1] Truth is engraved on a flat surface.

1. Subsequently published in *Transcript* (Dundee), Volume 1, Issue 2, 1995.

Reading Rooms. Janice Galloway, installation as part of the Writers' Reading Room at Transmission Gallery, Glasgow (1994), bed, bedside table and light, with texts and photographs

Rooms

extract from Reading Rooms

2

is a room full of beige flowers, tan leaves and orange stripes. The same wallpaper on every wall. Even so, the room hints at light. The curtains are white and fibreglass, semi-transparent in full sun: outside a washing line, a few tattie shaws in irregular clumps on a patch of earth. The washing throws shadows on the wallpaper jungle, drawing attention back inside. Maybe it's not so light as it first seemed. Posters of Doris Day as Calamity Jane, Claudia Cardinale, David McCallum, Davy Jones with his lips painted over in nail polish and Elvis in GI uniform (presented free with jackie) make dark blots on the nearside wall; a dull wooden wardrobe and a plain mahogany-tinted dressing table mar another. The wardrobe has curlicued legs; the dresser an ancient cylinder of talc, a brush and comb set, bits of glitter make-up and mother's red lipstick on a crocheted mat. Beige. The dresser mirror shows an orange bri-nylon bedspread and frilled

Reading Rooms. Janice Galloway detail of polaroid photographs

valance; the pillows do not appear until you turn round. Same colour and cloth, only quilted. Beside it, a cabinet shields Angèlique, The Practical Home Doctor and mother's wing-topped specs. The other side's study books (Primary Maths, Alice Through the Looking Glass with plasticine stains and a foosty smell to political philosophy and musical analysis texts — you choose) are simply ranged on the floor. A sheet with the beginnings of an essay hangs on one snapped sentence, waiting for someone to come back with a pen. Fragments of a male voice sift through the ceiling: THE OTHER CHANNEL MARGARET, SWITCH ON THE OTHER YIN, a comedy show laughing. At the sound of footfalls, the light fittings flutter. You know already, however long we wait, the televisions will grow no quieter. Look at the carpet again. Single sheets of piano score, shoes (sensible straps to platform leather thigh-boots — they've all been there), a hairnet crunched in on itself like a dead spider. Try how you might to ignore it, the focal point of the room is, however, the same. A fire vent over the bedhead. Its handle, waiting to open or shut the grille, glints a dull ceramic copper. Maybe it is already open (a sound like sore bones) in which case do not peer too close. Blue eyes will be apparent through the s-shaped slits, watching back.

The Year of the Letter. Jackie Kay, installation as part of the Writers' Reading Room at Camden Arts Centre, London (1994), table with eight books and poems

IN

extract from The Year of the Letter

The doors opened early and for one hundred and three years
the public had come in winter or summer, early or late,
wearing coats or jackets or hats to read the newspaper,
discover a family illness, or borrow a book for bed,
search the name of a rare flower,
or seek a book about a big bear who got lost, only
what was the name of the author?
To look up the Parish Register (Burials 1559-1883)
or find the telephone number of an old lover,
sit (unfit) in the Reference Room
reading *The Encyclopaedia of Swimming*
or sleep through *The Waking Dream.*

In and out she took the books, stamped with red ink dates.
Sometimes when she liked somebody she read everything.
From when she was a child. The smell of books.
The smell of silence.

I never go to the children's section,
all they've got is little women —
Heidi and Rapunzel, Anne of Green Gables,
when what I want is Lady Chatterley, Madame Bovary,
Hedda Gabler, Anna Karenina.
I always say, 'THESE are for my parents'
and use their cards (they never use them)
and that librarian with the cow-lick fringe
just blushes, stamps the book, no questions.

She found a relative in the Directory of Crematoria.
She found a novelist she would die for.
She learnt by heart the definition of claustrophobia.
She recited names in the local census (1881-1891) like incantations.
The M-Mortuary Drawer in Local History was a fatal obsession.
The syllabus for a course she never took lay in Universities, Box 7.
She looked tentatively into her family history, they were all mad as hatters,
She lived in the Book of Saints, especially the Seven Sleepers:
They were walled in a cave, the seven youths of Ephesus under Decius
(250) and were found alive in the time of Theodosius
(362). Saints all seemed to be called Catherine or Agnes.
The Furniture Beetle is closely related to the Deathwatch Beetle
from the Anobiidae family. Latterly she preferred beetles to people.
They could make quite lethal holes even in wood that is brittle.

Published in *Other Lovers*, Bloodaxe, 1993, ©Jackie Kay, first commissioned by Book Works.
For *The Reading Room*. The poems were placed between the pages of large illustrated
encyclopedia, left open on tables.

Something between my mouth and your ear
30 songs (from Jan-Sept 1966), cassette deck, amplifier, loudspeakers, blue paint, light filters

May, 1993
An organisation called Book Works contacted me. They are putting together a series of projects by artists and writers called *The Reading Room.* It sounds interesting. They want me to make something for them.
I say yes, I'll try. We talk about the various cities in which it might be possible to work; London, Oxford, and Glasgow. I don't want to work in Glasgow as that is where I live and I suspect people there are bored of seeing too much of me — enough already. I don't want to work in London as I've done too much there as well, although The British Library would be a good fun place to work, so I visit it, even although I don't think I'll end up making anything there. After this, I decide that I'd like to make something in Oxford.

I've never been there. I don't know anyone, and no-one knows me.

July, 1993
I make a first visit to look at various sites in Oxford; the Bodleian Library, Green College, the Ashmolean, the Radcliffe Camera and so on. I think Book Works want me to make an installation of text, something like something I might have done before; a critique on knowledge, power, and the literary traditions of the city, I suppose. They haven't actually said this to me, it's just a feeling I get. I don't really want to do this.

August - September, 1993
I've been travelling a lot, lately. This means I get the chance to read a lot more than is usual. But I am experiencing a strange kind of dislocation when I am in foreign countries and reading my books in English. During this time I'm reading Brett Easton Ellis, Jay McInerney, Donna Tartt and

Opposite: Something between my mouth and your ear. Douglas Gordon, installation at St. John's College, Oxford. Private Collection, London

some others from New York. Perhaps it is because of the narratives I am reading, but the voices I hear all around me are strange, and I cannot understand the majority of what is being said (I speak English only), and I feel slightly neurotic.

But the voice in my head, when I'm reading, is familiar even although I don't recognise it completely. This reminds me of something I read a few years ago in a literary journal, The Edinburgh Review. An Italian writer, Gianni Celati, was talking about the 'fact' that every time we read a word we hear a voice. We don't know where the voice comes from, but it is there, and it is the key to our interpreting a series of abstract marks on a page, recognising these as letters, which make words, then into some kind of structured sentence, and hopefully towards some kind of sense. It's a nice idea.

And then I start to wonder what kind of voice we hear if we read in a foreign language, or if we read a text by someone from another country. At this point you should try to imagine what is happening in my head; I'm a Glaswegian, reading American Psycho by Brett Easton Ellis, on a Korean Air flight, coming back from Japan, and on my way to Portugal.

Anyway, I start to get more interested in the idea of reading as an internal/aural activity.

December, 1993
Another visit to Oxford. I still can't decide on a site for my work — whatever it might be. But I make a decision that I don't want to tackle any literary or historical aspects of the city. This could be a problem for Book Works. I hope not.

January, 1994
I've decided that I want to make a work for *The Reading Room* which does not involve any reading (apart from these words you are looking at now).

I want to make something using sound; something between my mouth and your ear.

February, 1994
We decide to work at the Dolphin Gallery. It's small, and it's as neutral a space as one can use in a city like Oxford; no particular history to interfere with the work. Now I know what I want to make.

I'm going to pursue the idea of the reading room as an internal/aural space, and try to collate a series of sounds that represent this phenomenon. I try to think of the first sounds that I might have come across and where I might have heard them. I discuss this with some friends in Glasgow and we end up talking about the time immediately prior to my birth; these would be the months in which I would first encounter any received information. I begin to dig up as much material as I can on events between January and September, 1966. I visit the Mitchell Library in Glasgow and spend some time in the Music and Arts Reading Room where I discover they keep back issues of the Melody Maker, a music paper from the specific time I'm interested in. This is perfect. I begin to compile lists of songs from the 'Pop 50' as it was called in '66. There were some dreadful things in the charts during this time. I decide I have to be thoroughly subjective, which means goodbye to PJ Proby, Jim Reeves, and Tom Jones, among others.

The final playlist is:

the kids are alright – the who
turn, turn, turn – the byrds
I am a rock – simon & garfunkel

monday, monday – the mamas & papas
god only knows – the beach boys
I'm a believer – the monkees
here, there, and everywhere – the beatles
I want you – bob dylan

5d – the byrds
the sun ain't gonna shine anymore – the walker brothers
homeward bound – simon & garfunkel

last train to clarksville – the monkees
I'm only sleeping – the beatles
sunny afternoon – the kinks

pretty flamingo – manfredd mann
roadrunner – junior walker
paint it black – the rolling stones
summer in the city – the lovin' spoonful
my generation – the who
all or nothing – the small faces
she said – the beatles
8 miles high – the byrds
19th nervous breakdown – the rolling stones
sha la la la lee – the small faces

wild thing - the troggs
we've gotta get outta this place – the animals
making time – the creation
substitute – the who
under my thumb – the rolling stones
out of time – chris farlowe

March, 1994
I send the complete list of songs to Book Works and recommend the various pieces of audio equipment I think we should use. I also suggest that the room in which the songs will be played should be entirely blue.

Douglas Gordon, 1994

Silencium + Conservatory

Silencium is the title of a site-specific work realised at Transmission Gallery, Glasgow. An abstract concept shapes the discourse imagined through the regulations and tools present in a reading room. The guided and ritualised process of the acquisition of knowledge is here, manifest in the furnished conditions of learning.

Replaced by a screen, the 'catalogue' of a library contains a selection of phrases present in *Conservatory* at the Royal Botanic Gardens, Edinburgh.

The synthetic unity which is characteristic of all botanical glasshouses, their specific distance from reality, brought about by the exclusion of the socio-cultural context of those areas from which the studied plants are extracted, is the reflected subject of *Conservatory*. It illustrates the profound difference of two contrary systems of functioning; the linear, scientific thinking and the animistic cosmos of non-writing cultures.

During Western exploration and exploitation of Tropical rainforests, an exchange occurs which has dramatically resulted in a missionary desire to eliminate the unfamiliar or unknown, the unique character of a different habitat and culture.

Conservatory, presents an anthology of ca. 400 quotations and names selected from texts published during the last 500 years of Tropical exploration by the Conquistadors, explorers, botanists, entrepreneurs and anthropologists, for example: C.v. Linne, P. Löfling, C.L. Strauss, A. Bonpland, C.F.P. Martius, H.W. Bates, A.v. Humboldt, R. Spruce, A. Vespucci, R. Schomburgk, La Condamine, Nimuendajú, J. de Léry, H. Staden, N. Federmann, F. de Orellana, L. de Aguirre, Sir W. Raleigh, Prinz zu Wied, C. Columbus, Las Casas, Th. Koch-Grünberg, F. Carvajal, A. de Berrio, Ph.v.Hutten and A. Métraux and others. Engraved on labels which do not differ in type or shape from those which provide the Latin classification of the plants (species, family and geographical origin), they are displayed amongst the plants in four adjacent Tropical glasshouses. These texts symbolise the reservoir of knowledge kept in our libraries which provide a means of improving our awareness and understanding of the complexities and the needs of nature, leading to a realisation that we can and should change our way of life. L B

Conservatory was previously realised at the Cologne Botanic Garden in 1974

Left: *Consider the Lilies*. Elaine Reichek, installation at The Ruskin School of Drawing, Oxford. Photograph, pinstripe wool embroideries and embroideries on green, orange and white cloth, white lilies. Right: detail of lilies and pinstripe embroidery

Consider the Lilies

The installation in the Ruskin School of Drawing was a visual and literary exploration of certain trends in 19th-century British thought, which it set against broader, still-surviving historical patterns in Western culture — the patterns of attitude that led to colonialism.

The show began with a remark by John Ruskin, the founder and inspirer of the School: 'Remember that the most beautiful things in the world are the most useless; peacocks and lilies for instance.' The claim that the most beautiful objects are useless would seem to fall into the 'art-for-art's-sake' kind of defense of art. (The lily motif is used decoratively throughout the building).

In this exhibition, Reichek followed the use of the lily as a symbol in England's former, closest-to-home colony, Ireland, where in the same century that Ruskin was writing, the lily was gradually turning from an emblem of 'useless' beauty into a symbol of anti-colonial activism. This shift is charted in the shift evident from an early 19th-century poem, in which the lily is used as a political yet still aestheticized metaphor for the rebirth of Gaelic Ireland, to the lily's 20th-century status as a nationalist symbol, as shown here in an image of IRA Provisionals set against a wall painted with lily street-murals.

Certainly the miseries of war are never so bitter and many as when a whole nation, or a great part of it, forsaking their own seats, labour to root out the established possessions of another land, making room for themselves, their wives and children. . . . The merciless terms of this controversy arm both sides with desperate resolution.

—Sir Walter Raleigh, History of the World

When Elizabethans talked of colonies and of foreign planting they thought first not of the New World and Virginia but of Ireland—and Sir Walter Raleigh was no exception. Though history has rightly given him the credit for recruiting North America into the English speaking world, his settlements there were significant for their ambitions, not their permanence. It was in Ireland that he founded the plantations that . . . made his most substantial contribution to . . . England's overseas empire.

— Robert Lacey, Sir Walter Raleigh

In addition to the poem and the peacocks-and-lilies quotation, two more quotations from Ruskin appear: one in which the kindly-seeming aesthetician takes a genial, paternal, slightly scolding attitude towards the Irish colony, a second in which he more dogmatically and sternly makes a claim for the British equivalent of Manifest Destiny — the need to 'found colonies' so as to 'advance the power of England'. These quotations are machine-embroidered on green, white, and orange cloth — the colours of the modern Irish flag. There are also a number of further quotations revealing the similarities in attitude between the Englishmen who colonized Ireland and those who colonized North America, which are meticulously embroidered on charcoal-coloured, pinstriped, men's suiting cloth.

At the same time that the Ruskin quotations reflect his feelings for art, empire, and the Irish, Reichek's embroideries as a group suggested an alternative text to be read, an alternative history to be inscribed by a process of unravelling the weave of the male narrative.

Opposite: *Consider the Lilies* - Elaine Reichek. Detail of pinstripe embroidery

SUSAN BRIND AND JIM HAROLD
MYSTERIES OF THE HEART

'St James' Infirmary'
Sung by Louis Armstrong

I went down to St James' Infirmary
To see my baby there
Stretched out on a long white table
So cold, so white, so bare.

In this building the mysteries of the heart, the eyes, the limbs and the body can be studied one by one.

The Department of Human Anatomy at Oxford was originally built in 1892. Since then it has been extended several times. The inscription quoted is carved in Latin above the entrance of what was once the outside of the original building.

The photograph shows the physical space of inspection and analysis which surrounds the slate specimen table.

Permission was kindly given by Dr Charlton to photograph in the Anatomy Lecture Theatre.

St James' Hospital, which provides the original inspiration for the song *St James' Infirmary*, was founded in Norman times as a hospice for female lepers. In 1533 the site was purloined by Henry VIII and became what is now known as St James' Palace.

A number of variations of the song were made over the centuries in Britain and then later in the USA. The song finally entered the Jazz repertoire as a melancholic Blues number in the 1920s, played in the minor key.

Louis Armstrong sang *St James' Infirmary* many times. The version used here, copyrighted by Joe Primrose, was performed with Armstrong's Savoy Ballroom Five on 13 December 1928.

Opposite: *Mysteries of the heart.* Susan Brind and Jim Harold, installation at Camden Arts Centre, London framed photograph, etched glass tables, wall text

I went down to St James Infirmary

PUBLISHED WORKS

The spine of this pocket-sized paperback reads NOTABLE DAYS, but on its front cover, over what appears to be a distant galaxy with a dark centre, are the letters 'n.d.'; a bibliographic abbreviation for fugitive printed material that is 'not dated'. The rubric printed on the back of the book (which also serves as the colophon) dispenses with that strong convention of publishing that the date of appearance should somewhere figure. This is a book that aspires, as we come to realise, to the re-configuration of time and the calendar, within the printed space of pages and the imagined sequence of turning them. The rubric lays out the conventions which are to apply to reading the book:

For measures and dimensions, a day in this book generally means less than a second. A full year comprises almost any number of such days consistent with the decimal system up to and including ∞-1. An anniversary means the distance between one page and any other. Whenever possible, weeks conform to the present-day standard and are presented 'at a glance' and on the scale of the human body.

The images in this book are enlarged from newspapers; the insistent half-tone screen reminds us of this. Newspapers and the photographs repoduced in them can have a strong influence on the drift of history itself, and also, on the processes by which it is edited and remembered. Yet photosensitive newsprint darkens quickly and crumbles. Recent history and the present itself can be dark to us. Without access to a newspaper's thematic cuttings library or an information, search and retrieval system on computer or CD-Rom, history becomes what we can remember — or choose to cut out. Büchler has referred to the absurdity of the calculations that become possible with photography — the photo-yearbooks he has often used as source material represent 'no more than a few seconds' of the years they are said to represent, if one adds together the total exposure time of the photographs in them. The rubric of *Notable Days* asks us to imagine 'a full year' as composed of an infinite number of 'days'; it asks us to imagine a yearbook that admits of no physical limit to the number of pages, to the fidelity of its power to record. The weeks described as being presented 'at a glance' suggests a more intimate scale, a diary, a book in which we are to sign our names and make our own report.

The first half of the book comprises images of hands — which are indeed 'on the scale of the human body' — in relation to faces only parts of which are shown, and certain dates, the year not being given. Images of impatience or waiting, as if from a conference, interspersed with a repeated image of a crowd with flags, the wording of which is deleted and the colours, printed off-register, arbitrarily changed. The images in the second half of the book are drawn from photographs of the demonstrations in Wenceslas Square in Prague on December 14, 1989; a day which, with the other revolutions of that year, marks a point that has changed our entire perception of our times, the whole cast of our explanations. Francis Fukuyama and others were before long to publish their theses of an 'end of history' in which the final triumph of liberal democracy was announced. It's a notion that is invoked (or perhaps pre-emptively rebuked) by the text introducing the long section of the book consisting of dark images of crowds: 'At the end of seven days, Chronos died.'

As one looks through these indistinct images in the frame of a book, the stupid force of photography (the fact that all these people were there) recovers its power to shock. As an exiled Czech Pavel Büchler followed these events closely; perhaps it came as less of a surprise to him than to others that the Velvet Revolution, which seems in retrospect part of an inexorable process, was initially fomented by KGB provocation: inter-state interference that got out of hand, bungling that looks (from temporal and geopolitical distance) like destiny. In the book the tense approach to this moment is memorialised in imaginatively framed time-scales that are vast, dynastic and mathematical, but there are also indications of surprise and lack of ceremony: 'The next day arrived unannounced'.

Although some of the book's words invoke the historical attempts to juggle the calendar so that the cosmological and calendrical cycles tally — the attempt to get 'time' right — at its centre is a meditation on human actors, over a period of days and weeks. In *Notable Days* Büchler has made a powerful and evocative memorial to what we know of time: that things can go otherwise than they do, that the past is never wholly complete.

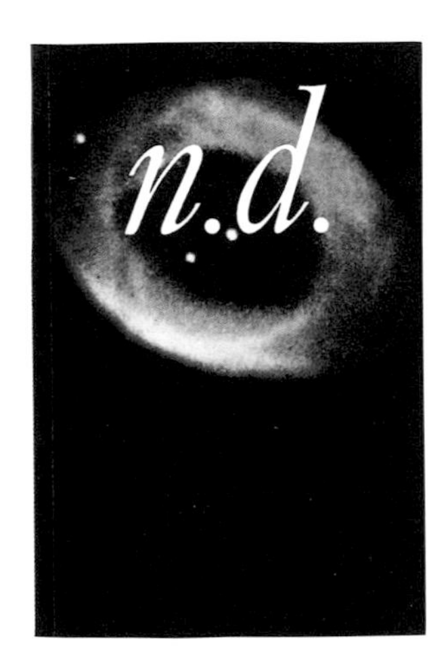

Notable Days

(not dated: published in 1990) 208pp, 215 x 145mm, printed offset on thin paper. Selected from open submission. Standard edition of 700 copies; a special, silver-edged, signed and numbered edition of 52 copies is 'offered for sale at the price of 12 troy ounces of silver each subject to the condition that they shall not, by way of trade or otherwise, be re-sold or exchanged except at the price stated above and based on the daily rate of silver at the time of purchase and without a similar condition including this condition being imposed on the subsequent purchaser'.

ISBN 1 870699 03 3

The Stumbling Block, its Index was described by Brian Catling as 'a direct attempt to write sculpture, to focus on an invisible shapeshifting mass, to try to see its contours, its material, its volume, in the different light of its manifestations'.[1] The promise the book's appearance makes to be the block is contradicted by the title, which indicates that what we hold is merely its 'index'. It is the first of a series of conundrums, such as the fact that the graphite-covered boards, which at first appear to be made of mineral ore, are soft enough to bear the embossed title (round like a company seal); and that the slightly greenish-grey paper, a heavy mould-made laid as used for ledgers and account books, bears no page numbers. 'The owner of *The Stumbling Block, its Index* has not merely bought a non-existent sculpture, but one whose non-existence is multiple.'[2] Although written in cadences that are definitively those of prose, not poetry, the cumulative effect of the

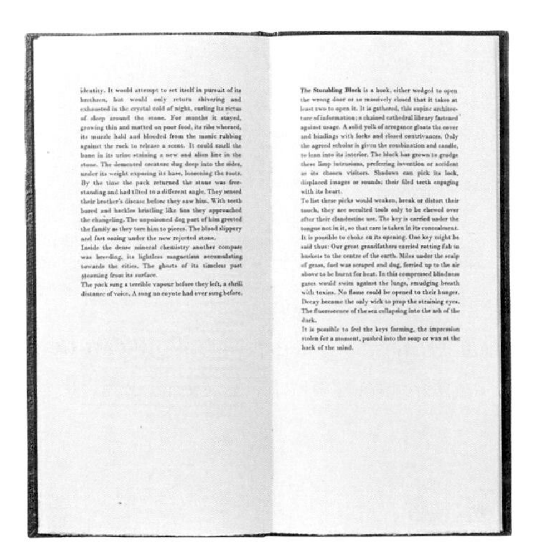

identity. It would attempt to set itself in pursuit of its brethren, but would only return shivering and exhausted in the crystal cold of night, curling its rictus of sleep around the stone. For months it stayed, growing thin and matted on poor food, its ribs wheezed, its muzzle bald and blooded from the manic rubbing against the rock to release a scent. It could smell the bane in its urine staining a new and alien line in the stone. The demented creature dug deep into the sides, under its weight exposing its base, loosening the roots. By the time the pack returned the stone was free-standing and had tilted to a different angle. They sensed their brother's disease before they saw him. With teeth bared and hackles bristling like fins they approached the changeling. The unpoisoned dog part of him greeted the family as they tore him to pieces. The blood slippery and fast oozing under the new rejected stone.
Inside the dense mineral chemistry another compass was breeding, its lightless magnetism accumulating towards the cities. The ghosts of its timeless past steaming from its surface.
The pack sung a terrible vapour before they left, a shrill distance of voice. A song no coyote had ever sung before.

The Stumbling Block is a book, either wedged to open the wrong door or so massively closed that it takes at least two to open it. It is gathered, this supine architecture of information; a chained cathedral library fastened against usage. A solid yolk of arrogance gloats the cover and bindings with locks and closed contrivances. Only the agreed scholar is given the combination and candle, to lean into its interior. The block has grown to grudge these limp intrusions, preferring invention or accident as its chosen visitors. Shadows can pick its lock, displaced images or sounds; their filed teeth engaging with its heart.
To list these picks would weaken, break or distort their touch, they are occulted tools only to be chewed over after their clandestine use. The key is carried under the tongue not in it, so that care is taken in its concealment. It is possible to choke on its opening. One key might be said thus: Our great grandfathers carried rotting fish in baskets to the centre of the earth. Miles under the scalp of grass, fuel was scraped and dug, ferried up to the air above to be burnt for heat. In this compressed blindness gases would swim against the lungs, smudging breath with toxins. No flame could be opened to their hunger. Decay became the only wick to prop the straining eyes. The fluorescence of the sea collapsing into the ash of the dark.
It is possible to feel the keys forming, the impression stolen for a moment, pushed into the soap or wax at the back of the mind.

book is neither. In a sense it is a riddle book, compacted from its own arguments between material and signifying processes. In that the Anglo-Saxon riddle book is too distant in time to be claimed as an ancestor, and the book wishes to own up to no secure resemblance to other forms, it seems more a forcing of the form of riddle book on a range of problems concerning spirit and matter, owning and not owning, the human and the inhuman — perceived as a problem of morality and cruelty and as a relation between the organic and the mineral. The historical parameters of these terms could be delimited, and their connections to specific forms of knowledge and assumption (popular science as well as theology, evolutionary pessimism as well as political economy) could be traced.[3] The following is rather a précis or audit of some of the evidence in the block's twenty unnumbered manifestations.

[1] 'is a graphite font': an electrical arc has played across its 'lips', and the block is associated with smelting and the generation of energy for turning wheels; it is now abandoned and gathers water.
[2] 'has been used like an entrance step to sharpen knives on'; the knives 'are magnetised to construct a lectern'. It 'may hold this index at its centre, hovering, placed outside in the aorta of streets'. 'Lectern' suggests, non-specifically, church or school. A street map that can sustain an image of the aorta suggests a large town or city.
[3] 'is an ark of extinction. A bouillon hive of the murdered past, frozen dry to a mass'; however, 'oxoed grit' bleeds 'contagion' from a 'warmed corner'. The block is an agent of species-catastrophe, emphatically that of homo sapiens rather than that of other animals.
[4] is 'unfound' but 'its nest, its negative hollow can be discovered in the mounds of waste and detritus that choke the streets'. It is also 'the light in the eye of the needle grown solid with anger, a fat sugar that clogs the passage to any kind of paradise.' There is no way to heaven for anyone, through any opening, probably because it does not exist; but the effect of this language tends to perpetuate the reconfiguration of existing circumstances as hell.
[5] 'is a bell that sounds a deeper voice than the throat of men'. It contrasts with their cult of speed and current technologies of communication (portable telephones, miniature televisions, satellites). It sweats, 'a human, modest sound that is unwelcome', whereas 'Tribes, villages, jungles and the very air itself can be wasted or burnt to secure a dry armpit'.

[6] 'is a shape shifter, a spirit bench that dwells in the cuffs' of a city described as 'expanding' though populated only by 'somnambulistic donors'.
[7] 'is a barrel organ dragged to the site of a crime'. Its music stimulates 'revellers' whose shoes are scuffed by dancing and which scratch 'cobbles'. Hazarding a date for this crime, one arrives at the nineteenth century at the latest, though the blood, one notes, has been 'soaked away' by laughter.
[8] is analogous to an art object but repeatedly refuses to submit in the customary ways (to money, bright lights, ownership). It is kin to an animal and 'will not be groomed for curation'. 'Its currency is elsewhere'.
[9] 'is an atlas swallowing its own tongue'. Catastophe — wind 'tearing the skin lamp-shade of Europe', floods which 'discolour the distinctions of territory and race' — is suggested and perhaps welcomed. While it breaks with the repetition of the past and announces 'another projection' this is presumably achieved at huge cost to the continuance of human muddle.
[10] is a dream of the block's 'possible paper heart of the forest of its origins'. The dream or reverie of the forest is disturbed by tiny falling objects, 'the coins of the poor'. Before hitting the ground they are transformed from metal alloy to an 'organic weight' and will seed and grow. Present inequality is magically reinvested in a forest, a place of 'origin' which absorbs the future 'miserable dormant past' represented by the coins/seeds, which by swelling into a 'primal eye' try to get evolution right this time.
[11] 'is a clock run on parable'. A case-clock, its (lead) weights 'classically inscribed *mercy*' were tied to the legs of a 'thin simple man' whose death they hastened. The second definitive crime, though this is by the state, which saw him 'sentenced for the malice of burning fields'. Unlikely to have taken place later than the nineteenth century.
[12] 'was once a rock in a desert, before it was cut and reshuffled its aim at the city'. It served as 'marking stone for wild dogs'. A sociobiological fable, with the attempted domestication of dogs representing a possible fall from a state of savagery/grace, into a period when human similarities with animals are customarily denied.
[13] 'is a book', though locked. The lock can be picked by various keys, one

of which is given to us and is historical. It is an account of miners, described as 'Our great grandfathers' who in digging for 'fuel', 'carried rotting fish in baskets to the centre of the earth,' that its phosphorescence should give safe light in 'areas of great gas'.[4] The other keys, 'pushed into the soap or wax at the back of the mind' suggest not only that knowledge must be stolen but also the doctrine of mind as initially a blank, a tabula rasa; a rather Cartesian or Lockean, seventeeth century idea.

[14] is again imitating 'a known thing', an art object; but here it is plural ('it or rather they'). 'They' are 'boards' once used for cutting up human bodies.

[15] 'has made itself of carbon paper'. The focus here is on language, scars, carbon (graphite, writing; also life and diamonds, which are invoked). As in [10] a semi-magical transformation back into origin occurs, from 'block to tablet', identified by Simon Perril as the root of book, the teutonic *bok* or writing tablet. Though the sense of judgement the block makes on present failures of communication is more telling.

[16] 'with some resentment shows itself as a television set'.

[17] 'suggests itself to become the conjuror's table'. It is concealed by a cloth, and offers no succour to the disappointed audience, robbed of a few coins. Nor can it 'respond to the pride of the conjurer'. The block's implied magic, like its 'currency' [8], is elsewhere, or has failed; it certainly has nothing to do with the conjurer's toys which include 'spheres of glass, rosy with dunce futures', a phrase that economically incriminates new age thinking and the commodity markets.

[18] 'is being hunted'.

[19] 'has become a pillow to the dispossessed'. Historical note: the book was selected from open submission. The suggested themes were contemporary. The dispossessed made a decisive re-entry to public life in the decade preceding this book's publication.

[20] 'is a night thing, that sits on the heart. It will sip from the ribs of guilt, to breathe luminous heat into flat shabby lungs elsewhere'.

1. *Soundings: A Tractate of Absence* (London: Matt's Gallery, 1991).
2. Simon Jarvis 'The cost of the stumbling block', *Parataxis: modernism and modern writing* 4, Summer1993, pp.36-41.
3. See also Simon Perril, 'A reading of Brian Catling's The Stumbling Block, its Index', paper presented to the Cambridge Conference of Contemporary Poetry, April 1993; unpublished, copy in Book Works archive. The text of the book has been reprinted in *Conductors of Chaos*, ed. Iain Sinclair (Picador, 1996).
4. Ian Hunt, 'An interview with Brian Catling', *Parataxis* 4 op. cit., p.42-57.

The Stumbling Block, its Index (1990)

Unpaginated (48pp), 255 x 125mm. Selected from open submission. Printed letterpress in Bodoni on Zerkall and case-bound at Book Works, with hand-worked graphite boards and embossed title. Published in an edition of 500 copies, with 25 special signed and numbered copies presented in a slip-case and containing an additional text handwritten by the artist.

ISBN 1 870699 05 X

The Blindings derives from similar impulses that led the artist first to write about rooms that served as still, exhibition-like frames for the aftermath of events that themselves evaded description. These fictional texts, *Written Rooms and Pencilled Crimes*, acted as a usefully ideal verbal challenge to a sculptor's ambition to actually make artefacts and rooms, use a variety of materials, to touch and manipulate. *The Blindings* describes works and performances that actually were made, revisiting them after the event in order to reconfigure them for the page as a modulated sequence of handwriting, description and print. Script is used for *The Blindings* texts, each of which contains a pronouncement that a fluid, gas, suspension or extract (urine, fluid from the antennae of ants, air, sweat, sap, a 'gruel of paper') has been injected into the eye, or that the eye has in some other way been deliberately violated. Perhaps it is too easy to say that this poetic strategy of imagined harm mingled with possibility is intended to renew or cleanse perception so as to understand something of the place it introduces. How could wishing do that? The texts are prayer-like in form, but this posture of prayer is halfway between horror and absurdity. The biblical cadence doesn't baulk at sliding into solipsism. In Nazareth, of all places, we read, 'I have injected my eyes with the oiled fat squeezed from the meat on my heated plate, in the company of my fellow travellers, that I might not recollect here so clearly'.

A solid type is used for the sections of the book that were actually spoken. This gives some of the sense of formality of the events where a repetitive cycle of texts were read out, as when *The Blindings* arrived at the Serpentine Gallery in London for a nine day season. These texts lurch from commentary on the place itself and its history, to recapitulation of the techniques, intentions and motifs of the sculpture. Speaking out loud is a peculiarly direct response to the limited attention that art can get, that by example establishes a different environment around the work, rendering it less precious or unique as an object (more like a prop to a performance) but encouraging sustained curiosity. This tames the concept of the artwork, and makes it a servant or vehicle, not necessarily of grace. An artist like

Catling, whose work is informed by knowledges connected to religion and mysticism, may in fact be playing with a semi-religious or magical expectation of art in order to demonstrate its failure and the richness of what comes after it; while forms of unrevealed religion can lurk in art objects that sit more proudly or smartly in the gallery.

Certainly the breaking of the taboo on speech in the presence of visual art, and the book's interest in using laughter, suggest that Catling is an iconoclastic artist. (In a Japanese shopping precinct he plays an ogre imitating a public clock's angel: 'He now also adopts the smile, a terrible thing when protracted across a human face, and begins to move in sequence with the automaton.') The other major durational piece recorded in the book, part of *The Reading Room* project, was that made for the Castle Mound, Oxford, where Catling read into a radio mike while pacing on the mound's top. The voice was broadcast into the stone chamber at the centre of the mound, in which there is a well. The texts Catling chose included the life of St Simeon Stylites, who lived on a pillar in Syria, texts written for the occasion and extensive cullings from *Stella C.* by Harry Price, an account of séances, in which lilac branches land on tables from nowhere and the temperature suddenly drops, and is recorded fastidiously by gentlemen with a thermometer. Catling's Reading Room was an imaginary vantage point in a city full of enlightenment, libraries and books, that chose to look in to darkness so as to sense and imagine extremes of experience: heat, cold, deprivation, hallucinations, emanations of psychic rods that one of the investigating doctors imagines operate on 'a cantilever system'.

Other works made by Catling for *The Reading Room* in The British Library are recorded in the book. A sound piece was broadcast to individuals only, who could access the work by applying for a special admission ticket for the Round Reading room, to sit amongst scholars to listen to it. Like the performance at the Castle Mound, this was an inturning work, though made and experienced in a large and echoic chamber.

The Blindings is a compendium. Its structure does not repeat but is newly inflected with each account, in order to make room for a variety of impulses, sublime and absurd. The images included are frequently oblique records of the performances they derive from; by asking the reader to construct their own images with the verbal accounts provided, Catling signals an explicit demand on the imagination, the image-creating faculty.

The Blindings (1995)

104pp, 200 x 156mm, published in an edition of 1,000 copies, printed offset, with a full colour soft cover and images in black and white.

ISBN 1 8770699 18 1

Scroll records a performance by Brian Catling in the King's Gallery at The British Library on the 19th of April 1994. 'It was a thirty-minute performance using amplified ambient sound, centred around a sloping-sided museum case filled with mirrored objects and condor feathers. The case was radio miked so that the performer could heighten the sound of touch and small whispers into larger distortions that filled the length of the gallery. Black ink in glass wells was used to bathe the performer's eyes into blindness.' Catling's performance persona here is of an over-grown, frustrated child, despite his slicked back hair and formal suit. The performer would have liked access to the objects in the case but found great difficulty getting into it, catching a button of his jacket, trapping his fingers. He tried to write with both hands at once and became pathetic with simple frustration. Having gained access, he bathes his eyes with successively stronger dilutions of ink. 'The performance ended after he exited through a hidden door in the book-lined glass wall, leaving only one hand tapping against the glass, like a skeletal fish.'

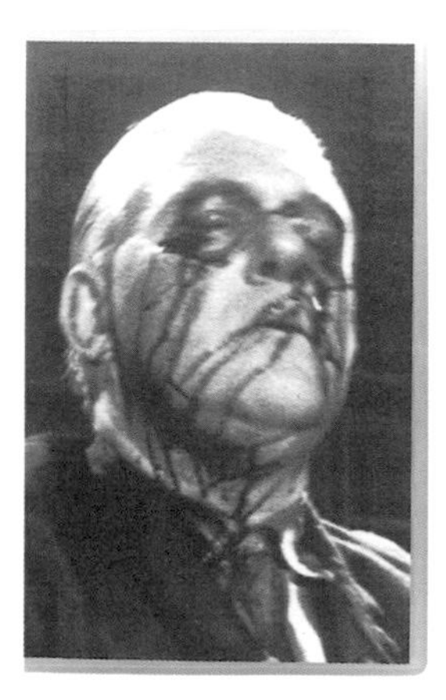

Scroll (1994)

Co-published by Book Works and The British Library. Video of performance by Brian Catling at the King's Library, The British Library (Length 15 minutes. Format: PAL-format VHS).

ISBN 1 870699 15 7

Jimmie Durham's *My Book, The East London Coelacanth, Sometimes Called, Troubled Waters; The Story of British Sea-Power* is animated by a distinctive voice — amused, obstinate and exciting our curiosity — that negotiates our and its own worries about what a book ought to contain, in what order, and for how long. *My Book* is what a proud eight-year-old might write; it's the first of many dares to make us think the writer naive. He attempts to present himself as a cocktail party bore, as a crank who would rather invent his own world-system than look something up in a book, but by the time we have worked out what he is getting at we start to wonder if we are that person not him. We know he is cleverer than this. We have heard about what he does, wondered what the dilemma of referring to him as Native American, Indian, or of Cherokee descent before (or instead of) 'artist' means — and have bought the book, or are at least reading it. But he will not out and tell us, will not answer the question, 'who are you?'.

The question is turned against us the (presumed English) readers and the book becomes a disquisition on the Angles, angling, a fossil fish, East Anglia, and East London, though this is not simply the place where the book itself was published but a town in South Africa, near which a coelacanth was caught in the 1950s. ('I have thought that, one way or another, if I could catch an East London Coelacanth in East London, England, I might somehow be helping resolve some of the residual problems of Anglish imperialism.') The accompanying photographs show Durham in various parts of the world, fishing or near water, and at different ages, and some other people with fish. Like the frontispiece with its shell or bone fragments and excited statement ('LOOK! THESE ALMOST FIT! I'M GOING TO LOOK FOR MORE!) they are another part of a puzzle that is not necessarily that of Jimmie Durham. Slipped in are two of an action by Durham in front of a railway arch/surveillance point, taken by Rory Poland, that the credits tell us is of 'Belfast and all Ireland'. Perhaps as a reminder that Anglo-Irish relations were a principal mental model for the colonists of North America, and that this history ought to be thinkable even if it cannot explain contemporary questions of national and ethnic identity and the severe problems they set.[1]

The book finishes before we are ready, at the point when the reader begins to get a sense of what its demands and its comic generosity are aiming at. It leaves a feeling that we had not read it properly and must now go back; its difficulty is that of *hearing* what the speaker is trying to say, and a feeling that if we fail to respond quickly enough or appropriately an angry or impatient response is possible. Anger only breaks out at one point, inflected with heavy New York irony: 'Often, when, instead of following the conversation you've been playing with a paper clip and someone says, "Do you think the Arab countries will come to Bosnia's rescue?", don't you feel just like a fish out of water? I mean, have we been here too long, and "Do I have to pay to keep from going through all this twice?"'

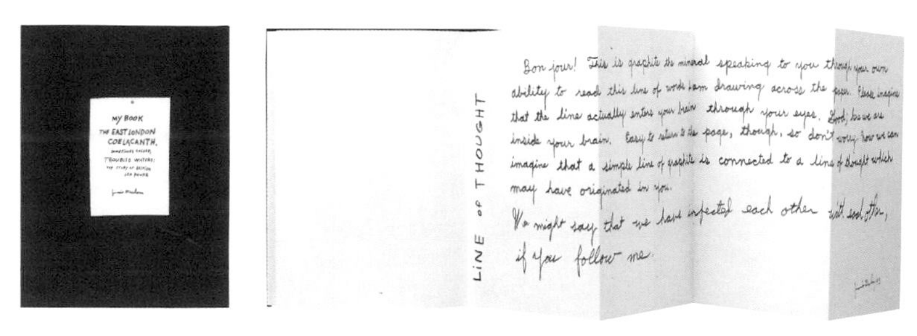

Books can be re-read; conversations cannot. The achievement of Durham's literary style is to remain close to the kinds of demands conversation can make on us while leaving the written record of approach, backing off and rapprochement which we can consult again, and which recounts a quest we are encouraged to imagine might be as much our concern as the narrator's. (Even the unorthodox type selected for the book, with small capital letters and large lower-case, emphasises this closeness to the vernacular, to speech.) Re-reading 'Metal fatigue and Social Politics', in which the smell of metal is explained, it seems that Durham's plan is literally to get up the reader's nose ('So where is your so-called personal "autonomy" then, Mr or Ms Bigshot?') but equally to point towards the constraints on any encounter beyond the control of either party, and to at least gesture towards the politics underlying them. On the first page of the book 'rejecting the physical universe (and its politics) of which you are comprised' is described as a 'Primal Sin'. This is a confident re-statement of a Marxist and internationalist position, despite the fact that position-taking as such is thrown into relief by what follows: a quasi-sermon that has Quetzalcoatl the Holy Dragon in place of Satan urging us to partake of the fruit of knowledge, a fruit that is difficult but in Durham's optimistic view, not impossible to share.

1. See Jimmie Durham's writings on art and cultural politics collected as *A Certain Lack of Coherence*, ed. Jean Fisher (London: Kala Press 1993) and the excellent study *Jimmie Durham* (London: Phaidon, 1995).

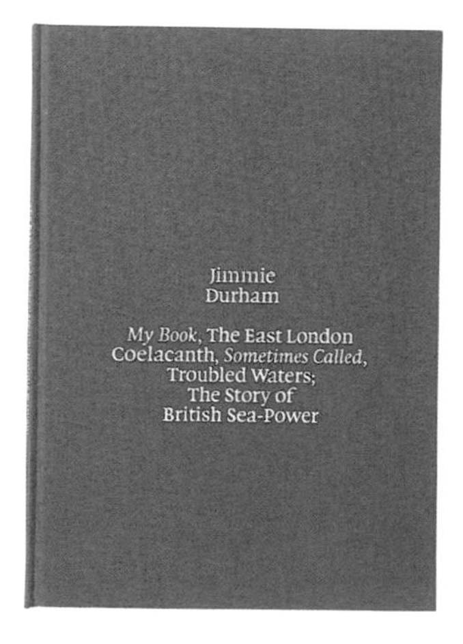

My Book, The East London Coelacanth, Sometimes Called, Troubled Waters; The Story of British Sea-Power

Co-published by Book Works and the ICA (1993). Text and images by Jimmie Durham with an essay by Dan Cameron. 48pp, 246 x 172mm. Printed offset in colour and black and white, and hard bound. Published in an edition of 1,000 of which the first 100 copies are signed by the artist. A special edition of 25 copies produced at Book Works contain an original art work by Durham.

ISBN 1 870699 12 2

The central character of this time-shifting narrative, set in London somewhere between the early nineteenth century and 1997, is late for a dinner party that he himself has planned. Although the West End streets and their electronics shops and night-clubs are unfamiliar territory for alternative history plots, some of the link lines are satisfyingly creaky: 'At this point we are still in a Georgian environment, so all of this analysis is still hidden behind a cloak of amateurism.' The characters invited are an odd bunch: Robert McNamara, Secretary of Defense under Kennedy; Elsie McLuhan, 'a public speaker specialising in moral tales' (and mother of Marshal McLuhan, the theorist of media, Catholic and cultural pessimist); Masaru Ibuka, co-founder of Sony; Murry Wilson, father of Brian Wilson whose group the Beach Boys he used as a vehicle for his own frustrated talents; and Harriet Martineau the writer and social reformer. The host is Erasmus Darwin, opium-eater and brother of the more famous Charles; who exemplifies for Gillick the activity of free-thinking. Although given the license to view the limitations of his historical experience in the light of later developments, Erasmus seems addled. Perhaps it's the drugs.

Freethinking is a form of political activity dependent on wealth and leisure that declares an uncomfortable relationship with 'unfree' thought and the classes which are or are described as unfree. Its primary interest for Gillick seems to be as an analogy for the precariously 'free' and disconnected potential of contemporary art, that sometimes seems to float far away from large-scale social movements and to function as the simple adornment of a culture it would rather have changed, and which it now doubts it can do more than puzzle. Gillick's book is born of such frustrations, but refuses to align itself with proscriptive solutions; Erasmus's final *cri de coeur* concerns a gap in which room to manoeuvre must be found: 'There's a difference between an administrator and a clerk. There will be a gulf between planning and practice. Use it.' By creating a main character whose chief activity is dawdling Gillick perhaps acknowledges that creative energy has gone astray, and that single-minded efforts to revive it without paying attention to the set-up in which it finds itself might not help.

Gillick doesn't miss the chance alternative history offers, however, to make use of provocative prediction. The introduction announces that circa 1997 the designation 'workers' (who presumed and fought for rights in employment) will be replaced by the term 'mob'; and mobs, while they had a certain warm and rowdy excitement, often proved malleable with gadgets such as bread and circuses, and in Britain, at any rate, have a tradition of royalism. (The presence of Masaru Ibuka of Sony in the plot is designed to suggest some contemporary factors relevant to this dynamic of control).

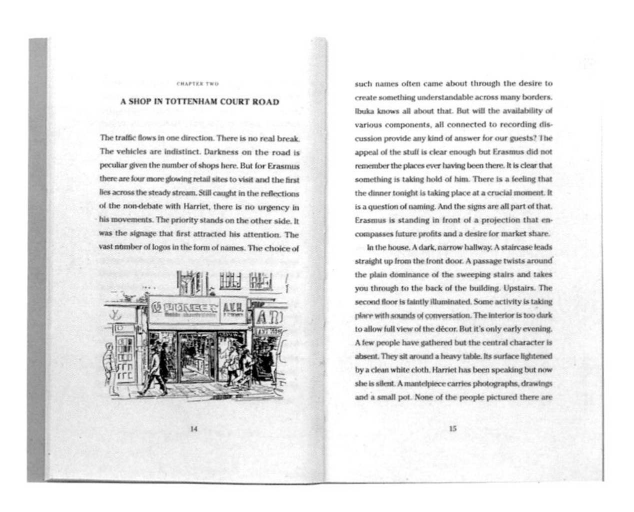

CHAPTER TWO

A SHOP IN TOTTENHAM COURT ROAD

The traffic flows in one direction. There is no real break. The vehicles are indistinct. Darkness on the road is peculiar given the number of shops here. But for Erasmus there are four more glowing retail sites to visit and the first lies across the steady stream. Still caught in the reflections of the non-debate with Harriet, there is no urgency in his movements. The priority stands on the other side. It was the signage that first attracted his attention. The vast nŭmber of logos in the form of names. The choice of

14

such names often came about through the desire to create something understandable across many borders. Ibuka knows all about that. But will the availability of various components, all connected to recording discussion provide any kind of answer for our guests? The appeal of the stuff is clear enough but Erasmus did not remember the places ever having been there. It is clear that something is taking hold of him. There is a feeling that the dinner tonight is taking place at a crucial moment. It is a question of naming. And the signs are all part of that. Erasmus is standing in front of a projection that encompasses future profits and a desire for market share.

In the house. A dark, narrow hallway. A staircase leads straight up from the front door. A passage twists around the plain dominance of the sweeping stairs and takes you through to the back of the building. Upstairs. The second floor is faintly illuminated. Some activity is taking place with sounds of conversation. The interior is too dark to allow full view of the décor. But it's only early evening. A few people have gathered but the central character is absent. They sit around a heavy table. Its surface lightened by a clean white cloth. Harriet has been speaking but now she is silent. A mantelpiece carries photographs, drawings and a small pot. None of the people pictured there are

15

In appearance the book is eccentric, and expresses Gillick's interest in making objects which appear to be from an alternative present. In a bright yellow wrapper, it is illustrated with line drawings (of various streets, shops and buildings refererred to in the narrative) by Gillian Gillick, the artist's mother. One of the questions this raises is why we rely on photography so much for our sense of what is contemporary; it is a real surprise to recognise contemporary west end shop-signs and the tunnels around Tottenham

Court Road Underground in the drawings. And the use by Gillick of the novel of ideas rather than the essay to express his interests is likewise oddly provocative. Gillick's work has often given the impression of withholding something; in grappling with the demands of a new form he has spelt out his concerns with new frankness.

Erasmus is Late (1995)

88pp, 180 x 115mm. Selected from open submission. Printed offset in an edition of 1,000 copies, with a soft cover and laser-cut title.

ISBN 1 870699 17 3

After the Freud Museum arose from the work made for *The Reading Room* project, a series of labelled, boxed works containing a wide variety of artefacts, texts and images, which drew a satisfying tension from their location, and carried the collective title *At The Freud Museum.* Hiller's brief 'notes on the plates' in the book help to position the reader as a participant. 'Sequences, patterns, repetitions and gaps structure this book. The not-said matters. A major factor in all the work I've ever made, it seems to me, is the designation of spaces where viewers and readers can experience their own roles as active participants . . . '[1] Though informative as well as anecdotal and personal, the notes always feel more than simple information ('Information is concerned with alien objects', wrote Hegel). Some seem designed to make us wonder at something unsaid: the motive for a journey to the cave where Aeneas descended into the underworld, 'near Vathia'.

The effect of the book is to encourage a fascinated, mobile attention that catches happily on the details of the separate stories we are offered and also registers the frustrations of what the collection withholds — the use of different scripts and languages in the titles, books that are carefully catalogued and rebound by the artist but presented to us unopened. *Simchas/Joy* contains copies of magic lantern slides, including scientific subjects and slides of early Disney cartoons which the artist found uncatalogued at the museum. We cannot view them — though they summon up the unforgettable image of the Freud family at home assembled around a screen in the dark. The accompanying table that classifies the subjects of the slides has a somewhat scientistic feel, and distances us from the contents again. As though to hold out the possibility of an intimate, tangible relation to myth or history and to withdraw it again, in a moment.

The work as a whole is a collection, but it is not clear that we can attribute obsession to it, as Freud's antiquities in particular make us think we must, or indeed impute Susan Hiller's ownership. Her work functions as a guide to some of its preoccupations, but it should perhaps be remembered that she once made a work called *Sometimes I think I'm a Verb Instead of a Pronoun.*[2] Some of the customised cardboard boxes archive or make reference to other works by the artist (*Bright Shadow*, a short video piece, plays on a miniature LCD projector in *Seance/seminar*; another box, *A'shiwi/native* recalls the shards of Pueblo pottery used in Hiller's installation *Fragments* . . . examples could be multiplied). But this does not close off the challenging range of questions the works provoke, from perception, intuition and other areas generally bracketed within subjectivity, to moments of historical crisis, questions of postcolonial politics, journeying and in particular tourism. This is a subject implicit in many of the collections: pigmented Australian earth, fossils from Mount Sinai, contemporary obsidian arrow-heads from Mexico, water from Ireland's holy wells, a miniature weapon bundle from Africa. Of this Hiller notes that it 'is so well made that possibly it should be viewed as an index to a complex tradition of skills and knowledge rather than as a meaningless souvenir for tourists.' One wants to know more, specifically where and when made, but the title, *Provenance/source*, acts as a brake. The rush to classify, like the rush to pronounce on the deleterious effects of globalisation, disables our ability to see what might be happening, what accommodation of differing forces artefacts can contain.

As Hiller notes notes in her afterword, 'Freud's impressive collection of art and artefacts can be seen as an archive of the version of civilization's heritage he was claiming; my collection is more like an index to some of the sites of conflict and disruption that complicate any such notion of heritage.' Language is inescapably part of this picture. In *Pâinjenisul Satanie/Satan's Cobweb* we encounter the mapping of the phrase 'ethnic cleansing' onto an earlier period, via Hiller's finding of an illustrated book on the persecution of the Jewish minority in Romania. The archaeological aspect of the project — that these material objects have been retrieved so as to be held up to the light, that the past (and aspects of the unregarded present) speaks through them — abuts the evidence of language's role in that retrieval, as that which can reveal but also petrify meanings and explanations in the sediment of usage. (It is no longer useful to keep our distance from the phrase ethnic cleansing by means of inverted commas, but the familiarity with which it is reached for has its own bitterness.)

After the Freud Museum has the disquiet and appeal of rumour, a proximity to the imaginative usefulness of the outdated and the mythical — like the illustrations of pregancy in ten stages lasting ten lunar months, rhymed with ten miniature porcelain cups. (Each child, after all, repeats and never quite discards mythical ways of thinking about the world.) In moving easily between the generalized and the personal, poetic logic appears to be running behind some of the important stories of our time, while not wishing to concede them everything.

1. Some recent approaches to Hiller's work can be found in the catalogue published by the Tate Gallery, Liverpool, 1995; Michael Corris's essay 'Susan Hiller's Brain' published in Susan Hiller (London: Gimpel Fils, 1994); and in 'Immigrant' a long text/commentary on *At the Freud Museum* by the anthropologist James Clifford, published in *Sulfur* 37, Fall 1995 (Ypsilanti: Eastern Michigan University).

2. 'From this position the "subject" is not fixed, nor the predicates accidental: they acquire their meaning in a series of relations to one another. Only when the lack of identity between subject and predicate has been experienced, can their identity be grasped.' Gillian Rose, *Hegel: Contra Sociology* (London: Athlone, 1995) p.49. Hegel might also be brought in on the question of classification itself: 'What results from this method of labelling all that is in heaven and earth with the few determinations of the general schema . . . is nothing less that a "report clear as noonday" on the universe as an organism, viz. a synoptic table like a skeleton with scraps of paper stuck all over it, or like the rows of closed and labelled boxes in a grocer's stall. It is as easy to read off as either of these; and just as all the flesh and blood has been stripped off the skeleton, and the no longer living "essence" has been packed away in the boxes, so in the report the living essence of the matter has been stripped away or boxed up dead.' (Preface to *The Phenomenology of Spirit*, Miller trans., p.31.) It is, I would argue, by so fully engaging the 'deadness' of ownership inherent in systems of formal classification (as opposed to the poetic or associative kinds, including the relationship between myth and place), that Hiller's archive reflects the artefacts collected back into life, understood as a dialectical moment that renders the histories both around and sedimented in them perceptible; or at least summoning a sense of what that would be like.

After the Freud Museum (1995)

114pp, 302 x 175mm, printed offset in an edition of 1,000 copies, illustrated throughout in black and white. Hardbound in a specially designed cardboard binding resembling the collecting boxes, with inset photographs and blocked titling.

ISBN 1 870699 19 X

Residue (left over)

A multiple published in an edition of 10, was produced and printed by hand at Book Works to coincide with the publication of the book. 'Quotation from Walter Benjamin; artificial corsage, made in 'USSR occupied' Germany, labelled and tagged, in customized cardboard box, labelled' (255 x 330 x 65mm).

In the preface to *Reading the Glass*, the three editors describe the book and how we might approach the content: 'This book occupies an uneasy space. It is neither academic text nor artist's book and yet shares something with both. It might sit on a shelf or be equally appropriate in a pocket. It might remind one of many things — missal, rhetorical guide, a treatise on aesthetics. If it belongs in no one place, well, that is somewhat its intention — a kind of homelessness. Its beginning rests, with greater certainty, in Rome in the spring of 1990; from conversations held round a fountain in a courtyard, in the sun. Our interests linked, casually at first, overlapped, became eventually this book, and all the variations on this book which precede the one you hold now in your hands.'

Book Works' initial commission had been to publish a book with Sharon Kivland, who in turn invited eleven others to contribute to it. It is this ability to collaborate with others, artists and academics alike, that has become one of the key-notes to much of Kivland's work, whether it be in the form of published works or exhibitions, and was to provide the starting point for this book too.

Reading the Glass addresses the question of the gendering of the gaze through a series of words and images, exploring the act of looking, illustrating the difference between the male and female gaze, and speculating on whether a space that is not gendered can exist within an image, within language. The book has a structured feel to it, and is sub-divided into chapters that each contain a dialogue, with the gendering of the gaze under discussion: throwing into question the boundaries of numerous discourses: verbal and visual, male and female, academic and artistic.

The editors in turn, invited eight people to contribute to the book, grouped into pairs, woman-man, and artist-theorist, although in the preface they note that these categories of practice swiftly collapsed. Each pair enter into a dialogue with each other through image and text; the sections are self-contained but each has a complex relationship with the overall design of the book. The rich form of the book, designed by Sue Foll, also suggests many voices, using different papers, typefaces, gold blocking and colour, giving distinct textures to the commentaries and dialogues running throughout.

Three chapters are given a specific gender: 'Cyclops' represent the male gaze, described as 'monocular, phallic, self-regarding'. In this chapter accounts of the historical Cyclops (some of them extremely brutal) from Ovid, Homer and a Turkic source, *The Book of Dede Korkut*, are placed opposite texts of a quite different kind: 'Consequently there is need of constant management of the eyes, because the expression of the countenance ought not to be too much altered . . . it is the eyes that should be used to indicate the emotions, by now assuming an earnest look, now relaxing it, now a stare, and now a merry glance, in accordance with the actual nature of speech.' Taken from Cicero's manual of rhetoric, the contrast of this 'management' with the spontaneity of the Cyclops itself is striking. The second chapter 'Medusa' draws on images of woman and the mirror — a trap for the gaze — and questioning it.

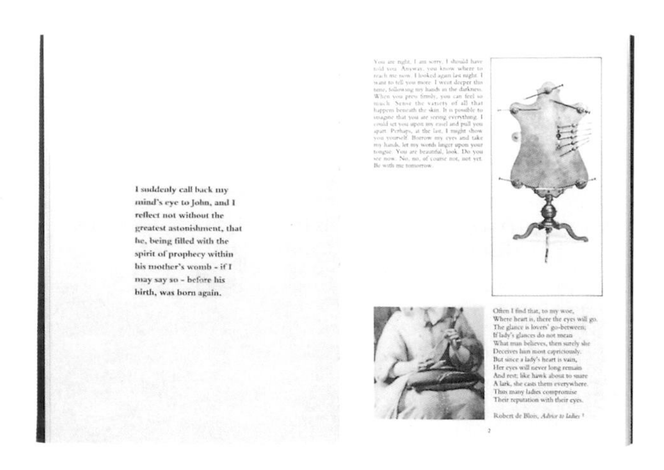

The third chapter, 'A Love Letter' which falls between these two, is a speculation on whether a space that is not gendered can exist, within image, within language. This last chapter is positioned in the centre of the book, though the editors suggest it is read last, and it is here that the reader is asked to draw his or her own conclusions — 'It is a letter to a third party, who, like desire, is always elsewhere.'

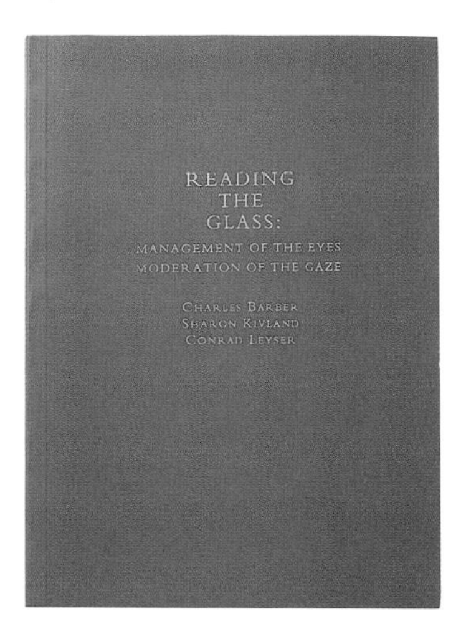

Reading the Glass: Management of the Eyes, Moderation of the Gaze.
Edited by Charles Barber, Sharon Kivland and Conrad Leyser (1991)

Contributions by Silvie Bélanger, Lorenzo Buj, Nina Danino, Liz James, Forbes Morlock, Michael Punt, Susan Trangmar and Wes Williams. 144pp, 215 x 150mm. Printed offset in black, white and colour, with foil blocking on the front cover and central pages. Published in an edition of 600 copies.

ISBN 1 870699 08 4

Sharon Kivland's interest in Sigmund Freud, and her close reading of his 'Fragments of an Analysis of a case of Hysteria, (Dora)' (*Standard Edition*, Vol III, London, 1953) have resulted in a number of works over the last few years, including *J'appelle un chat un chat.*

Published in an edition of ten, the book contains an extract of text from 'Dora', followed by the names in French for ten shades of red lipstick, that might equally be read, without prior knowledge, as referring to states of emotion or female attributes: *Essentiel, Symbole, Rayonnant, Audacieux, Flamboyant, Fou-rire, Sanguine, Tabou, Imaginaire, Diabolique.* In addition to the text are ten mounted photographs of different women wearing the different shades of red lipstick; each book in the edition has a different image. The edition has been sumptuously produced, printed in black, and shades of red, bound in black calf leather, with distinctive white lettering and presented in a black, felt-lined box, with a hidden layer containing the glass-mounted photograph.

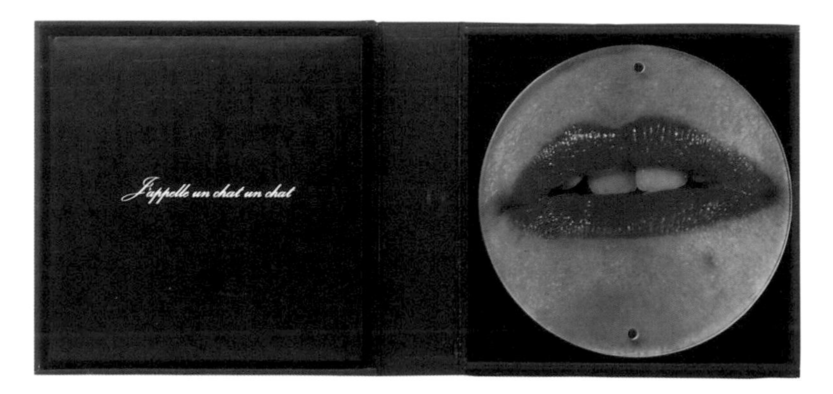

A video work also accompanies the book. This video has been produced by Shelagh Wakely in response to *J'appelle un chat un chat*, and provides a dream-like quality which matches the mood of the book: 'I watched the pages of the book turning on the monitor and listened to the rustling as the evocative words, the names of the lipstick were revealed.'

The book has a sensuous nature in the use of materials, the way in which the text reveals the image, and the double meanings at once banal and deeply serious. Freud's own text reveals his intentions to speak frankly and scientifically on matters of sexuality and the female body, and then at the very point of speaking directly, appears to hide behind a vulgar euphemism — J'appelle un chat un chat. It is this displacement that Kivland was keen to examine, and commenting on a larger installation, which included elements of this work, says: 'I want to draw attention to the meaning that is both simultaneously suppressed and accentuated, and must remind you that the divan of the psychoanalyst is replaced by the couch of the boudoir.' (*Aphonia*, Editions Centre d'art plastiques de Saint-Fons, 1994).

J'appelle un chat un chat (1994)

34pp, 190 x 190mm. Published in an edition of ten copies, hand printed letterpress in black and ten shades of red and bound at Book Works. The binding is in black calfskin, with circular photographs mounted under plate glass, each is signed and numbered by the artist and contained in a drop back box.

ISBN 1 870699 16

J'appelle un chat un chat (1994)

A video by Shelagh Wakely has been produced in response to this book and the first ten copies of the edition are signed and numbered by the artist and presented as part of the limited edition book. (Length 11 minutes. Format: PAL-format VHS).

Joseph Kosuth made two installations in Oxford as part of *The Reading Room* Project, for the particular contexts of the Taylor Institution and of the Divinity School of the Bodleian Library. This book reconfigures those works back to back; *The (Ethical) Space of Cabinets 7 & 8* is printed vertically, while *Say: I Do Not Know* is printed horizontally. The colophon page, unusually, is in the middle of the book, together with a selected list of previous works by Kosuth which show the context of these works within others, over a period of thirty years.

The (Ethical) Space of Cabinets 7 & 8 puts in apposition extracts from texts by Voltaire and John Locke, interleaved with photographs of the glass-fronted cupboards in the Voltaire Room, which hold editions and translations of Voltaire's works, contemporary desk diaries used by the library for administrative purposes, microfilm of an edition of his works annotated by him and — no explanation is forthcoming — boxes of reproductions of printers' woodblock ornaments, and heterogeneous Voltaire material including an LP of the Bernstein opera *Candide* and cassettes (stuff libraries find troublesome to store and categorise). Interleaved are tracing paper pages, on which the texts are printed, so as to make in the frame of a book an effect similar to that of the installation, where the texts are screen-printed on the glass doors. Cabinets 7 & 8 are empty, and make a different kind of context for the ethical questions arising. For Locke ethics (and the arena of action) is only reached after the cautions of epistemological reflection, but is in a sense radically separate from it; the relationship between knowledge and action is a troubled one. Voltaire, who admired the English philosopher so much, emphasised his contribution to the understanding of religious toleration, and himself took a more active role in politics and public life.

For Cabinets 7 & 8 the quotation from Locke that has hitherto been repeated is replaced by two other extracts, and the final extract from Voltaire has an urgency that threatens to escape the hush of scholarly labour with a sudden and clear contemporary relevance: 'Do you realize, for instance, that at this moment there are a hundred madmen of our species wearing hats killing, or being killed by, a hundred thousand other animals wearing turbans, and that over almost the whole face of the earth this has been the custom from time immemorial?' The powerlessness of both art and philosophy before such 'custom' can make philosophical and aesthetic scruples seem precious and perilously disengaged. And yet the demand for 'action' in the political arena so often turns into the pressure to deliver, to be seen to do something rather than that the something done is appropriate, adequately prepared or just. Kosuth's work is prepared to take the risk of appearing to stand back from the arena of action and ethics precisely because, like philosophers, he is prepared to question the terms with which engagement is made.

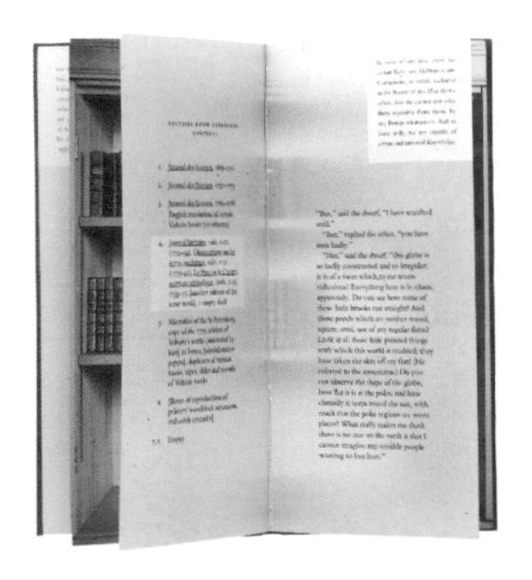

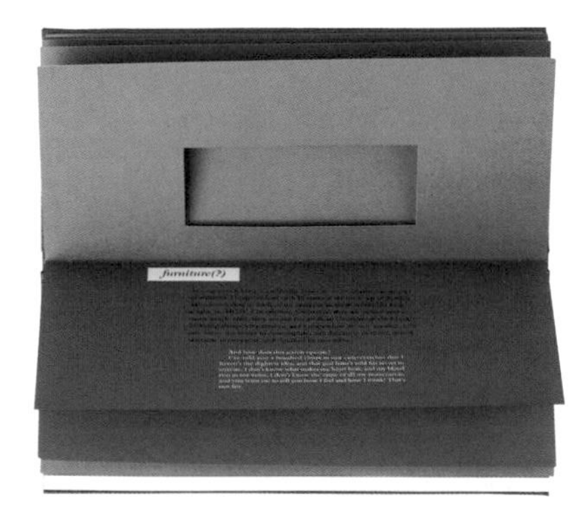

Say: I Do Not Know concerns the nature of images and of signification. A single quotation from Locke's *Essay Concerning Human Understanding*, is visible through a die-cut hole in the page, and is repeatedly contrasted with differing extracts from Voltaire, many on the question of idols and statues in Greek culture. The extracts from Voltaire are written on the Socratic model of the philosophical dialogue, which enacts the production of meaning as the disagreement, move and counter-move of two speakers (and serves, perhaps, as a model for Kosuth's understanding of the 'Play of Art' in its institutional setting.[1] For Locke, the patient analyst of the social agreements on which meaning rests, the possibility of disagreement was fearful. Yet his accounts of habit, language, and of personal identity frankly exposed, amongst other things, the arbitrariness at the heart of the signification process itself, which has been so debated in linguistics in this century. He did this not in order to erode meaning, but to promote the possibility of agreement effected on a reformed basis. The extract from Locke's *Essay* repeated by Kosuth concerns 'collective Ideas', the reality of which Locke does not dispute, though he wishes to make clear what kind it is: 'They are but the artifical Draughts of the Mind, bringing things very remote, and independent on one another, into one view, the better to contemplate, and discourse of them . . .'

The extracts from Voltaire approach the issue of signification in relation to representations of gods: 'What view did they then take of the statues of their false divinities in the temples? The same view, if I may say so, that we take of the images of the objects of our veneration. The error was not to worship a piece of wood or marble, but to worship a false divinity represented by this wood or marble.'

Selective citation unlocks these arguments from their context, and creates for them another one, which is framed first by Kosuth's title *Say: I Do Not Know*. Its personal pronoun is uneasy of reference. It seems to be a statement offered to the reader to speak; like the words followed by bracketed question marks on the pages, it necessarily affects the tentative approach made to interpretation of the texts. And if the repetition of Locke's words on 'collective Ideas' carries some weight in the book it is perhaps because the passage from singular to plural, from I to we, is partially effected in the way the uneasy personal pronoun of the title brings the plural readership of the book tentatively into view — without the coerciveness that so often accompanies the use of 'we'. What constitutes 'knowledge' in the appositions of *Say: I Do Not Know* is thus governed by neither an 'I' nor a 'we', and is distanced from an obvious set of names or readily appropriated representations. By contriving a sense of the signification process that is palpable (the play of each move and counter-move as one turns the pages) the book makes a specific, artistic contribution to the questions it asks its readers to consider.

1. *Writing, Curating and the Play of Art*, Joseph Kosuth's lecture for the Reading Room Symposium, is published as a pamphlet by Tramway, Glasgow in association with Glasgow School of Art.

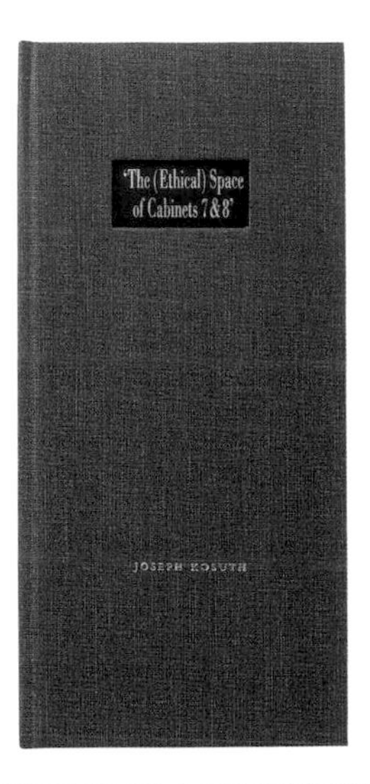

Two Oxford Reading Rooms (1994)

Published in an edition of 1,000 copies as part of the Format Series, 112pp, 98 x 210mm, with a special hard bound edition of 250 silver-edged gilded, signed and numbered copies, case-bound by hand in linen boards at Book Works, presented in a slip case. The book has two distinctive front covers, and each element works towards the centre of the book. Printed offset in white, black and grey, with cut-outs on inside pages and covers.

ISBN 1870699 14 9

The Price of Words has a similarity to two of the archetypal forms of the book: the alphabet book from which children learn to read and the book of memory, which nowhere exists but has so often been imagined as fundamentally entwined with the function of writing. The book's subtitle, 'Places to Remember 1-26' links the alphabetic plan of the book to the injunction to remember, so important in Judaism and Jewish culture. The 'places' are pages of the book, though reference is made within them to actual places — lived in, moved from, arrived at, passed through, never named or identified.

The alphabetic section of the book is prefaced by black and white photographs showing sand pouring into a metallic bowl, or spilling across its rim (these images preceded an installation of a similar form made for *Book Works: A Women's Perspective* in 1992). The grain of the photographs shows, and they are taken at different shutter-speeds, sometimes capturing the motion of the grains of sand and sometimes letting it accumulate into a blur. It is not always clear whether one is looking at a positive or a negative, at stillness or movement; these perceptual paradoxes being germane to a book that ends 'I ask you what you cannot read — read'. Any book that contains words, however carefully chosen, can provide such a strong framework for interpretation that the effect of the images may be diminished. In *The Price of Words* the near symmetrical structuring of the book — which includes two empty openings and prefatory quotations from Kafka and the poet Erich Fried — encourages a repeated process of comparison, of doubling back and re-consideration, of images as well as words. In the last image in the book the bowl appears almost empty; it is as though the 'flow' of sand is in reverse. Turning back to Kafka's aphorism, we read,

'Never will you draw water out of the depths of this well.'
'What water? What well?'
'Who is asking?'
Silence.
'What Silence?'

The book is not a work of straightforward memorial observance. It addresses the question of how different generations of Jews work through the need to forget as well as to remember; the artist's parents, 'who in their lonely and decrepit days, break out into the languages of their childhood,' must necessarily measure the price of words and language differently than she does.[1] Memory is finally identified (in the entry for letter Z) with 'becoming' and with an orientation to the future. Though the book collates some pages that are blank and in its shifts between visual and verbal, engages with muteness (the injunction to read what one cannot read) it is not finally content with silence.

1. The phenomenon of the return of childhood languages in old age is movingly recounted in Gillian Rose's philosophical memoir, *Love's Work* (London: Chatto & Windus, 1995).

The Price of Words, Places to Remember 1-26 (1992)

60pp, 200 x 155mm, printed offset litho in an edition of 500 copies, with images printed in duotone and a fold-out pictorial cover.

ISBN 1 870699 09 2

A parlour game said to be practised in literary circles is called 'Humiliations'. To take part, one must confess the titles of significant books one has not read. The curious thing is that humiliation ceases to be the point rather quickly and bravado display takes over. Should one confess that one has not read Rousseau's *Confessions*, on which Jeremy Millar's *Confessions* appears to be based? Moving on from these uncertainties, the conduct of Millar's narrator, if we are to believe what he writes, gives an account of the transformation of faux-naïveté and embarrassment into ambition and display that is compact, funny and troubling. The process of repeating an earlier writer's thoughts and words has produced something more chillingly original, for whatever that old chestnut is currently worth, than many a contemporary tell-it-like-it-is narrative. If compared to those examples of the confession genre that litter newspapers and seem to have become the journalist's standard way of setting out their wares, the book makes clear a surprising cultural development: the death of shame. Perhaps the book is a perverse plea, if not for the reintroduction of shame then at least for an understanding of what it once meant to be ashamed. The narrator, by his lack of sympathy with the idea, makes its usefulness clear.

'This was not my first time in Italy.' We are introduced to a man travelling with a married couple he is not sure he likes. (In gold type on the back of the book, or rather 'volume', we read 'If one wishes to devote one's books to the true benefit of one's country, one must write them abroad.') But we have failed to read the first page properly. He is not travelling, but recalling a former journey, of which the entire book consists, as it were in parenthesis; the implied second journey to Italy is never recounted. We read on, fascinated and appalled. The man's ambition rises with each step though he aims strangely for a monastery, where it takes a more-holier-than-thou aspect. Intrigue follows him. 'I broke free from his clutches with a cry; although I had no idea what was happening, my surprise and disgust were so visible that he then left me alone. But as he let me go, I saw something white and sticky shoot from him toward the fireplace and fall upon the ground.'

Worse follows. A priest explains that to be found attractive in this way is not to be taken as an insult. Do we believe in the narrator's supposed innocence? Do such novelties never happen in Switzerland? Do we believe in his scandalous portrait of the Catholics whose religion he adopts? (Croats, Africans and Italians on the make in a cosmopolitan proto-sauna, with lots of ceremony and dressing up: this excess will surely lead back to Protestantism, where disgust at the body finds itself at home).

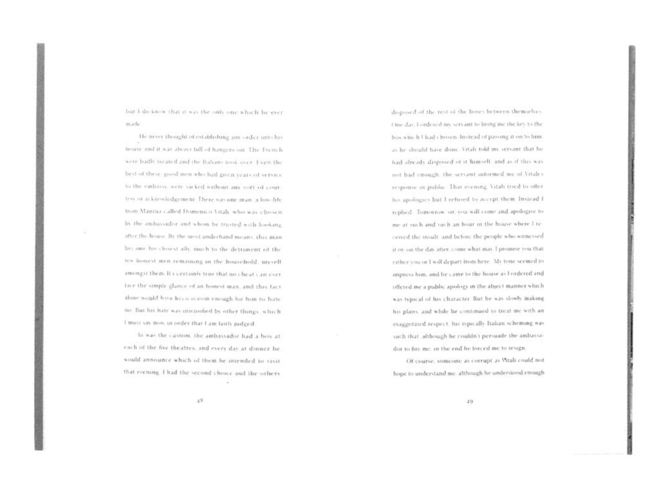

but I do know that it was the only one which he ever made.

He never thought of establishing any order into his house and it was always full of hangers-on. The French were badly treated and the Italians took over. Even the best of these, good men who had given years of service to the embassy, were sacked without any sort of courtesy or acknowledgement. There was one man, a low-life from Mantua called Domenico Vitali, who was chosen by the ambassador and whom he trusted with looking after the house. By the most underhand means, this man became his closest ally, much to the detriment of the few honest men remaining in the household, myself amongst them. It's certainly true that no cheat can ever face the simple glance of an honest man, and this fact alone would have been reason enough for him to hate me. But his hate was intensified by other things, which I must say now, in order that I am fairly judged.

As was the custom, the ambassador had a box at each of the five theatres, and every day at dinner he would announce which of them he intended to visit that evening. I had the second choice and the others

48

disposed of the rest of the boxes between themselves. One day, I ordered my servant to bring me the key to the box which I had chosen. Instead of passing it on to him, as he should have done, Vitali told my servant that he had already disposed of it himself, and as if this was not bad enough, the servant informed me of Vitali's response in public. That evening Vitali tried to offer his apologies but I refused to accept them. Instead I replied: 'Tomorrow, sir, you will come and apologise to me at such and such an hour in the house where I received the insult, and before the people who witnessed it or, on the day after, come what may, I promise you that either you or I will depart from here.' My tone seemed to impress him, and he came to the house as I ordered and offered me a public apology in the abject manner which was typical of his character. But he was slowly making his plans, and while he continued to treat me with an exaggerated respect, his typically Italian scheming was such that, although he couldn't persuade the ambassador to fire me, in the end he forced me to resign.

Of course, someone as corrupt as Vitali could not hope to understand me, although he understood enough

49

With sufficient Italian to write letters for a dying Countess, the narrator encounters self-propelling greed in the servants and hangers-on, and notes that this will aid him in his dealings with the scoundrels he is to encounter in Venice, where he is bound. But there is something not quite the ticket about him. He has started to expose himself to farmgirls. What does it mean to say, let alone write and publish such things? W.S. Graham wrote in *What is the Language Using Us For* that 'Certain experiences seem to not /Want to go into language maybe/ Because of shame or the reader's shame.' The behaviour is unspeakable; therefore to confess it is to brag, to abuse the reader as a confessional, which is in any case a sordid piece of furniture. The truth or not of the statements is not the point; to confess or to lie with such fastidious carelessness is the highest sign of disrespect to the reader.

Did no one explain to him that if you cannot think of anything to confess, the priest will offer a list of suggested sins?

In Venice, the narrator gains employment in the French Embassy, learns the ministerial cipher, and institutes a pious reform of the procedures for issuing passports: a perfectly comprehensible and locally acceptable system of bribes, grace and favour. His reform is designed by the moral opprobrium he bears towards everyone; he knows in advance that they are all lazy, stupid and corrupt. His citadel of self-esteem seems unbreachable. 'I was alone, without friends, advice or experience, in a foreign land, and in foreign service, surrounded by undesirables who, for their own interests and in order to prevent themselves being shown up by my example, urged me to do as they did.' Like a jumped-up civil servant, he recounts every petty victory and, when things start to go badly, every slight and insult. And then he burdens us with his cultural observations, and cannot even tell us that he learnt to overcome his Parisian prejudice against Italian music without explaining, with cock-eyed logic, that this was because he was fortunate enough to have been one of those born to understand it.

Unconvincingly shameless to the end, the narrator manages to break his ritualistic self-abuse for long enough to have some affairs. The climax of one is his evident unhappiness with any form of reciprocity, which by his willingness to confess he sets in stone and justifies. 'Though she was beautiful and charming I could just about put up with losing her. What I cannot bear is that she left with only bad thoughts of myself.' Her deformed nipple was too much for him, though she had accepted his unusually shaped penis without a word — as far as we know. The engraving of a (male) chastity belt on the cover of the book says it all: this sex toy heightens a pleasure that will never allow itself to be shared.

Jeremy Millar's repetition of *Confessions* performs the useful task of reminding us what ugly characters have been elevated to the Penguin Classics list. More precisely, it poses the centrality of disingenuousness in contemporary life: the careless lie, the careless truth.

Confessions (1996)

84pp, 210 x 150mm Published in an edition of 1,000 copies as part of the New Writing Series, edited by Michael Bracewell and Jane Rolo, printed offset, with a full colour soft cover.

ISBN 1 870699 21 1

At the other end of artist's book production than many of those described here, Avis Newman's *Supplement* was an opportunity for an artist whose work has persistently focused on the relationship between description and knowledge to address those concerns in the form of the book. The book is informed by all aspects of her work. Newman's paintings hesitate before the act of description, the marks moving in and out of a referential function to human or animal forms, frequently against pale or white backgrounds, employing marks which may dissolve to describe light or stain. In a recent series, *Webs (Backlight)*, layering of paint over graphite marks has been employed to evoke the central emphasis of spiders' webs: which are both a bodily product and a form that is (perplexingly) one of those which seems a form of natural design or proto-drawing.[1]

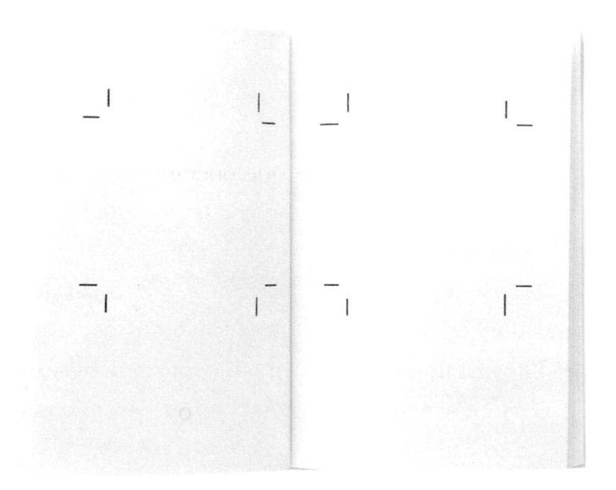

The beauty of Newman's paintings is not, however, part of a cult of the ineffable. The constructions, boxed and framed works represent another side to Newman's interests. By their titles and conceptual play with container and contained (salt, pebbles, even a polished block of wood can be boxed and framed), they deflect interest away from the centre, occupied by something queasily natural or unaltered, to the heavily worked frame. The printed pages of *Supplement* play with the possibility of translucence in ways similar to the paintings, while its form as a boxed object that negotiates the strong conventions of printing, publishing and illustration connects it to the more overtly linguistic investigations of the constructed works. Its heavy slip-case, coated in granular, dark red *caput mortuum* pigment, offers another clue. *Caput mortuum* (Latin — dead head) is the name for a synthetic iron oxide, but it is also an alchemical term for the residuum remaining after the distillation or sublimation of any substance. ('Good for nothing but to be flung away, all vertue being extracted,' the O.E.D. records from 1681.)

The book's scale and preciousness, with its cover wrapped in glassine and fine letterpress printing, makes turning the pages into a highly self-conscious activity. It is the kind of book which demands to be studied at a table with sufficient room and has a peculiar power to define the atmosphere in which it is consulted. The book is uncut, and is printed on smooth, mould-made paper; nevertheless it permits what printers call 'show through'. Because the pages are uncut one sometimes cautiously peers at what is printed on them from the side openings, before examining the effect of how deep one can read 'in' to the book without turning a page. The translucence of the paper makes many unsuspected combinations of the few elements of the book. Thirteen of these uncut pages are printed with the marks used by printers to indicate where a page is to be trimmed by guillotine. The first three of these are not numbered, but an empty circle (in the same position as that on the cover) and a quotation are visible on other pages underneath them. 'We write, as we paint, with, ivory black which, as you know, is the fine black powder obtained by mixing ivory with burned bones.' Needless to say, the book is printed in black ink; the colophon does not reveal the recipe used. The quotation is followed by a finer, larger circle printed in the centre of the rectangle defined by the cut-marks, and then by the words FIGURE. The final ten rectangles defined by cut marks are numbered 0-10. It is here that one cannot be sure how far one can see into the book and starts to imagine that the accumulated printing of ten sets of marks (all defining the same rectangle, but varying slightly in length) must render the thickness of the book visible.

A leaflet issued at the time of publication states that 'the book's title suggests it is both additional and complementary to an unspecified thing, the shape and content of which can only be presumed through an inspection of the constituent parts.' Curiously, the book's determination to avoid some forms of definition does not mean that familiarity with the 'unspecified thing' is quite impossible. The longer one stares at the parameters for existence it may have, the more the promptings of the printed marks (and their alliance with burned bones, with cutting) become guides to naming it as 'the thing not yet named'. *Supplement* is a figure for an incorporation into language, however difficult, traumatic or hyperbolic, which necessarily cuts into the chilly ineffability of that which it would hold.

1. See *Avis Newman* Ikon Gallery, Birmingham/Camden Arts Centre, London, 1995.

o

Supplement (1993)

48pp, 290 x 195mm. The book is uncut, printed letterpress (in Albertus on Zerkall paper) in an edition of 70 signed and numbered copies, with a paper binding and a glassine wrapper, and is presented in a slip case pigmented with caput mortuum.

These three books have been produced by Chris Newman as a series. They all share something of the same character, yet subtly develop and possibly become more resolved as 'published' works with each edition. Newman is an artist, musician, composer and poet, and brings these attributes in equal part to the book page. The work has an elusive quality to it, and may surprise the reader by its refusal to be classified or tamed.

In his book, *Eugene Dubnov Poems 1979-90 by C. Newman*, an accompanying text explains something of the nature of his poetry: 'It is almost impossible to get around and it is consciously or unconsciously intended: the hyphens liquidate the lines, which are quickly used up; apparently they must quickly give way to new ones. These separations become the theme — short, brutal separations, naturally those of the flesh: from excrement, from a lover, from the passage of time. At the beginning of each fresh chapter (each line) a brief wish to set out, the rover's passion. The author as a monosyllabic hero, as a hero of the monosyllabic. Life, existence, and fate as brusque counter-attackers. The fundamental impulses of the text, both its allure and danger, are as short as a dog's bark.' [1]

The books work as a series of openings, arranged in a sequence that builds up a complete narrative, through gesture and repetition, with the printed text revealing something more of the content in its staccato presentation: the content is derived, as Newman himself puts it, from 'a time spent on trains between London, Cologne & Paris . . .'

The limited number of copies in each edition, and the seemingly random edition sizes, point to the fact each book is made as a monoprint, printed by hand, with pencil and ink drawings, colour foils and texts layering the work. Newman works on the edition in an automatic but logical way, from a plan. Like any 'improvised' work of confidence, the work has its own particular and intricate idea of structure and movement around and sometimes through fixed points. Each copy of the edition is based on the same plan using words and phrases to create images, continuously overlapping, building up a rhythm, until a conclusion is drawn. And the edition is adjudged complete. If the books can appear to be a series of images, with their sumptuous painterly use of texture and colour, then it is through the printed end-text and also through Newman's performances and readings that one can measure the weight of the words and phrases.

1. Essay by Jürg Laederach from *Eugene Dubnov Poems by C. Newman*, published by Edition MusikTexte, Cologne 1993.

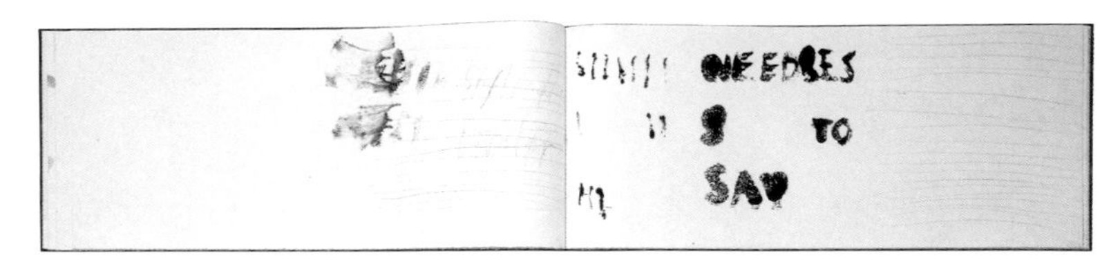

Me
Life is held on rather than repeated
Not repeated
Not repeated
Danke schön
Cross out the page
Never heard of them
Unimportant but light
Service
Downhill thrill
Shit 3 times in the night
-ness
Hope
Hoop
Heart
Hook
Drink
Drink
Hope
Fuck
WC
Gravity
Water Kills
I walked it
Tongue up cunt

(extract from 'Me')

If Road was Rubber (1990)

The book is produced, printed and bound by Chris Newman and Book Works, with an average of 32 images in each book. The pages are designed to open as single spreads, folding at the fore edge. It is case bound with a printed canvas cover and presented in a drop-back box. The box measures 380 x 270mm. Published in an edition of 20 copies.

Book No.2: The Moon and the Stars (1991)

The book is produced, printed and bound by Chris Newman and Book Works. It has 24 pages and measures 330 x 760mm. It is casebound with a printed and hand painted cover and presented in a drop back box. Printed in an edition of 17 copies signed and numbered by the artist.

'Me' (1993)

The book is produced, printed and bound by Chris Newman and Book Works. It has 56 pages and measures 230 x 305mm, is casebound with a printed cover and is presented in a slipcase. Published in an edition of 27 copies signed and numbered by the artist.

Cornelia Parker's work is based on a notion familiar in twentieth century art, the transformation of objects by the artist's nomination of them for our attention. What is striking in her work is a palpable interest in how material transformation, very often a process of destruction, can release the associations objects may have for us in a very direct way. The stuff of the everyday world and from the lumber rooms in which material history is locked up escapes, and the commonplace poetry of things is given back to us. It's a project with deep affinities to the still life tradition, but animated by a sense of derring-do excitement and by sculptural interests in gravity, lightness and weight. (A related work to *Lost Volume* was the crushing of numerous metal objects under a steam-roller, *Thirty Pieces of Silver*. The objects were presented in galleries suspended on long threads, so that they floated six inches above the ground.)

Lost Volume, A Catalogue of Disasters explores what happens when the three dimensions of height, depth and breadth are crushed to two, the realm of representation and the printed page. The book records the crushing of objects in a press between sheets of heavy paper, and the embossed indentations created. Each opening of the book captures the surprise and the delighted possibility of disaster of the moment when the blankets of a printing press are peeled back. Symbolic destruction does mean, however, that the objects are definitively presented for reading, flattened for the page; and they have an emblematic quality. A box of Swan Vesta matches; a company of lead soldiers; a trumpet; a trophy; a medal (showing the abraded head of George V); black grapes; a cash box; a Christmas tree decoration; a dried starfish; a tube of printing ink; some Cream Crackers (the pale wording on which is still visible); a pre-war tin globe; a clear glass lightbulb. Recognition of these objects is not always easy, and the contents pages (at the end of the book, like the solution of a puzzle) show pictures of the objects in their intact state. It also shows some other objects, including a ring and a cigarette case dated '1917', which are not to be found in the book elsewhere; there is no explanation, but their inclusion here perhaps indicates that simple destruction is not the only way of losing things the book recognises.

Any artist who makes work that appeals to child-like instincts runs certain risks. Childhood cannot be raided to revive dulled adult habits (in this instance, how we relate to objects) without a certain perplexity at what we are to do with delight when it has been recovered. There is a danger of burning our fingers — as we first did with the forbidden matches like those on the cover of the book. By selecting objects that seem to have a particular historical range and provenance Parker alerts the reader; details that may have been magical and mysterious to a child are to the adult eye markers of British and imperial history. The crushed globe and lightbulb at the end of the sequence perhaps suggest lights out for old ways of thinking about the world. This book recovers an undeniable pleasure in the gleeful moment 'what if' but also registers its awkwardness for us; and the complexity of decisions about what we choose to keep and what to throw away.

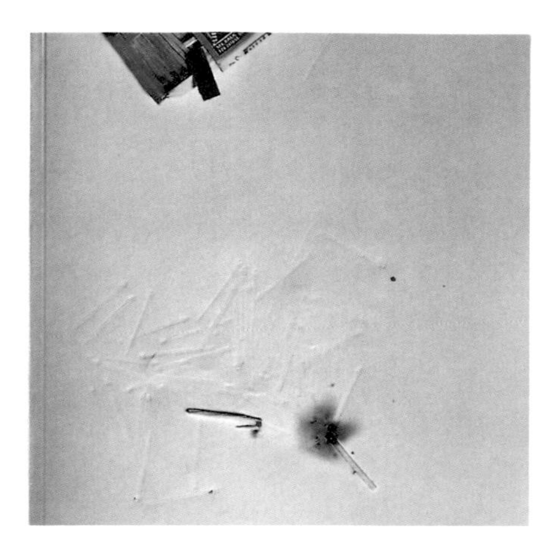

Lost Volume, A Catalogue of Disasters (1993)

32 pp 245 x 250mm. The book is printed offset, with a full-colour soft cover. Published in an edition of 500 copies, with 30 special signed and numbered copies including an object that has been effected by the artist, and bound by Book Works. Photography by Edward Woodman.

ISBN 1 870 699 11 4

This small book's clarity of presentation and its format, perfectly fitted to the hand, suggest that it aspires to usefulness, that it should be kept ready to be consulted in case of difficulties. Its contents belie this innocent demeanour. The contents page of *Rex Reason* informs us that this is a book of elements, from 1-107, and introduces us to the colour-coding system (black for solid elements, red for gaseous, blue for liquid and yellow for synthetic), but flicking through the book we have already found that the letters that serve as chemical symbols for the elements have been used as the source for an association game. Ge, Germanium, with an atomic number of 32, is paired with the name Pietro Germi. Yb, Ytterbium, atomic number 70, has suggested Yul Brynner. The methods of association start to become clear: the letters of the chemical symbol must occur in the same order in the name chosen, though not necessarily consecutively. (So Zirconium, Zr, can suggest Zoltan Korda.)

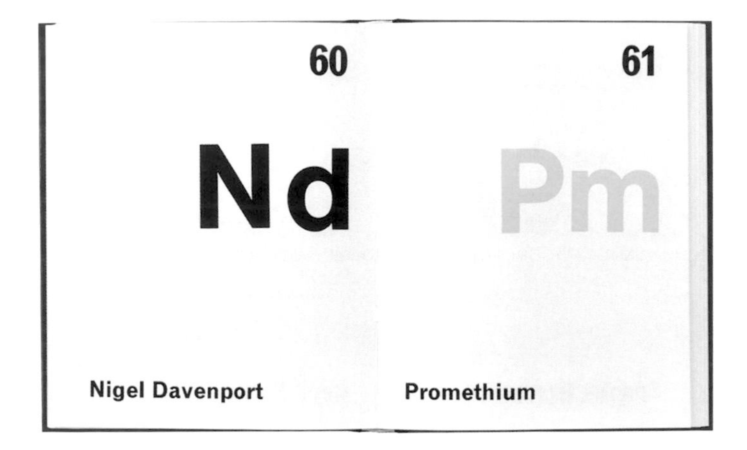

The book has already introduced us to two nagging problems, however. The first is that the source used for the associations, the Periodic Table, is less familiar to us than we think; and the abbreviations are often based on the elements' chemical rather than common names. The names selected, likewise, are often elusive. Pietro Germi, for example. Did he design cars, have something to do with the Nevada Project, or could he conceivably have given his name to the germ? And it must be faced: names announce a cultural origin, and those formed in unfamiliar ways are harder to remember than we would sometimes like. The colour coding helps with some of the business of classification and sorting into sets, but not entirely. Names in black (solid elements) seem to be mostly film stars, directors, and entertainers. Names in red, gases, are from Greek myth or history. Names in blue, liquids, of which there are only five, comprise Galileo Galilei (Ga, Gallium) Bertolt Brecht (Br, Bromine), Maria Callas (Cs, Caesium), William Hogarth (Hg, Mercury), and Fra Angelico (Fr, Francium). Patterson's particular heroes, perhaps, and evidence of favouritism disrupting his system. Investigating the elements themselves in the hope that the characteristics of a set based on some other principles can be found may not help. Scientific naming principles will be revealed by any reference book as excessively whimsical: Gallium, for example, was named after gallus, Latin for cock, after its discoverer, Lecoq de Boisbaudran. Presumably because Lecoquium was thought an undignified name for an element in 1875.

Any attempt to pin down Patterson's logic seems likely to fail, but neither do his interventions side so firmly with the forces of disruption that we feel inclined to give up: his book is called *Rex Reason*, after all. This is made most clear by his treatment of the synthetic elements, coded radioactive yellow, which increase in frequency as the atomic numbers get larger — and give the book its plot. These elements are all allowed their proper names: Technetium, Promethium, Curium, Bilkolium, Californium, Einsteinium, Fermium . . . right up to the latest to be synthesised at the time of the book's publication, Unilhexium (107). This appears, after the other sets' engagement with myth, art, and entertainment, to be a celebration of scientific progress, a homage to the particle accelerator. One by one the unstable elements whose structure has been predicted have been created and their existence has been documented, at least for a split second.

Patterson's treatment of the synthetic metals, however, proves that he has made use of at least one red herring that can be classified as belonging to that species: Bilkolium (Bk). But this does not mean that he is making fun of science, or of the reader's (evolutionary) wish to establish meaning and pattern in data (even if sometimes we feel that it escapes us as surely as control does from Serjeant Bilko). Berkelium (Bk), we establish, is actually named for Berkeley, California, where so many particles have been accelerated. In Berkeley, and in labs everywhere, the search for red herrings and unforeseen variables in data is part of what science is, and how it evolves as a fully human activity. Patterson's light touch in this book is not a joke that closes a process of investigation but a wit that inaugurates it.

Rex Reason (1993-1994)

Rex Reason is the first in the Format Series of artists' books published by Book Works. It was originally produced as a single presentation copy for the Arts Council Award for the Prudential Arts Awards in 1993. The Format Series edition consists of 2,000 copies, printed offset, 116pp, 105 x 130mm, soft cover.

ISBN 1 870699 13

Rex Reason (1993-1994)

The special signed, numbered edition of 10 copies is printed letterpress, and hand bound with a leather spine and a perspex cover, and is presented in a clothbound box. It measures 205 x 260mm.

'Tickled pink. Scarlet with embarrassment. Purple with anger. Blue. Green with envy. Jaundiced yellow. White with fear. Black depression.' Adrian Piper's book is a collaboration with sixteen people, whom one is forced to sense as 'people' from the moment one reads the title, which is printed with a black outline coloured in red and green. This simple tactic makes the eye pause; but even as some thoughts become focused, others don't. Is the expanse of white that makes up the cover a colour too, or is it just a background?

The participants were asked to act out the 'metaphorical moods' and to send photographs of themselves, which Piper took responsibility for sorting, according to her response to the expressions. The book was first produced as a mock-up for a travelling exhibition in 1987: *Women of Color National Artists' Book Project*, and as Piper writes in her introductory note to the book, 'was intended as a lighthearted conceptual gesture with serious implications'. As the project proceeded, the seriousness of the collaborative aspect of the book itself emerged more forcefully, what the implied contract between the artist and the participants actually involved. The thirty-six participants originally invited to take part included equal numbers of women and men, 'people of color and euroethnics', though the sixteen who agreed naturally didn't.

'First my collaborators had to trust me not to use their images in a way that would make them look bad or silly. That is a hard thing to do in a profession that perceives success as a zero-sum game, in which one person's benefit is another's disadvantage.' The photographs are arranged in sections under the heading of the colour moods, and the faces are coloured in, as though with pastel. This serves a double function: to enhance the mood that Piper has categorised (which the participant may perhaps have thought represented a quite different feeling) and also to half-obscure the faces. Many of the participants have, in any case, covered parts of their faces, closed their eyes and turned away with evident caution before the cold lens of the camera. Many seem barely to change their expression. Like any collaborative project, the book turns out to be a commentary on democratic participation and its limits. The goodwill may not have vanished when the time came to fulfil the obligations of the agreement, but producing emotions to order for publication clearly provoked some uncertainty in the participants' minds. (An important right in any democracy is not to have to take part, or to dissent at the forms that participation may take.)

The overacting of the emotions requested turns out to be another way in which the participants 'evaded their brief'. To turn oneself into a caricature of a mood such as fear makes the real fear that may actually be felt illegible, guards it in private. And there are reasons to guard feelings in this way. The main way in which the book is received, in the context of Adrian Piper's work as a whole, is as a commentary on the speed with which race, sex and class inform our behaviour towards others, and continue to structure our perceptions especially of those whom we don't know. The book does more than simply repeat this implicit challenge to readers to assess their response to others, however. Race, sex and class, because they are so often repeated together in this triad, are identifiable in advance as part of a formula. Ah-ha! Politically correct art; summon up appropriate angry/self-congratulatory sentiments. *Colored People* is a project that attempts to deal with two aspects of pre-judgment; those made about others and those made about art that is delimited as political as a method of containment of what else it may be about, how richly politics may be defined.

'There's no art/ To know the mind's construction in the face.' The relative willingness to feel or give outward sign of feeling is idiosyncratically distributed amonst men and women, all of whom make their choices on the basis of the customs and conventions available and adapt them to their needs. A complicating factor in this — in relation to art dubbed 'political' — is that there has been a demand for narratives in which individual evidence and experience of the varieties of inequality is made to conform or exemplify generalised patterns. The demand is usually made for good reasons — generalised patterns are useful tools — but within these forms individual experience finds itself, sometimes, estranged again, become emblematic. *Colored People* turns out to be preoccupied by neither generality nor individuality, but to be a collective expression that, with each turn of the page, shows the resistance offered to producing shows of feeling on demand. It is not always possible to express oneself or give another an outward sign, even when one may want to, and it is safe to do so; these reluctances too are shades of feeling that make their own demands.

Colored People (1991)

292pp, 280 x 215mm. The book is printed offset litho in black, white and colour, and has a soft cover with a printed dust jacket. Published in an edition of 1,000.

ISBN 1 870699 09 2

To err is to hesitate; and then to make a mistake. In David Shrigley's understanding, mistakes are necessary, and are going to happen in any case; so the point is to get some in first. *Err* begins with a listing of 'complaints' received after a previous book was published, which includes 'Errors of a moral kind (too much evil on one page, etc.)', and goes on to explain that 'what follows is an attempt to highlight these errors for the benefit of those who tried to read the first volume'.

The book bristles with all the proper apparatus a book should have: glossary, bibliography, notes on contributors, though the style is that of unauthorised activity: vandalism and graffiti. (The 'further reading' includes 'swearwords written in the dirt on the side of the bus.') The author's note reads: 'I am an authority on dirt and filth. I am an authority on bad weather. I am an authority on meanness and cruelty. I am an authority on worried children . . .' The tone never becomes self-satisfied; Shrigley's works wrest from these things a desperate laughter and make us feel, for as long as we can bear to read, that his bleak view is not something peculiar to a diseased mind but a version of the brutality of everyday life in Britain that might actually be true. And because it deals with things we don't like to acknowledge, Shrigley's work has a compulsive quality, a furtive, pornographic fascination. Once you have started laughing at his captioned drawings, anecdotes and absurd tests and puzzles, you want more, you want it to happen again. A page headed 'His show was no good' depicts various semi-art activities ('Heads on spikes on the city walls — oh please! It's so sixth-form . . . Public hanging — he's obviously desperate to please . . . A fire-breathing dragon — entertaining for the kiddies maybe . . .' The last item on the page is an indecipherable mess, captioned 'Small, delicate models of ships etc, stamped on, smashed, ruined — now this is pretty good'. Shrigley's drawings often take this form: a set-up which once entered can only be left by the violence of a rule change we wish for but can't quite predict. By reading this far we are virtually committed to enjoying a moment of violence.

Perhaps one of the keys to Shrigley's accuracy is that his tests, puzzles, primitive systems of classification and brutal appositions (things that come in threes; suns and burns; games won and lost under the microscope) demand small, irritating tasks of interpretation, and set up absurd constrictions which we give in to; but which are more like the kinds of decisions we are faced with and the thoughts we are occupied by on a minute-by-minute basis than we would like to admit. Like advertising, the dominant form of the picture-puzzle, which occupies our minds with the morsels of thought required to link words and pictures, Shrigley's work can seem an inept set of wagers to take up our time when we know the result may be facile. It exposes our sheer willingness to play according to rules we did not ask for, in the hope of small rewards. 'TIME TO CHOOSE' announced an early Shrigley drawing, of an angel, a devil and an nebulous figure above the words GOOD, EVIL and DON'T KNOW respectively. We cannot choose to ignore the command; non-cooperation is allotted its box to tick. The point of Shrigley's scrawled style becomes clear. When feeling faced with such choices, the only means of expression left is to spoil the paper.

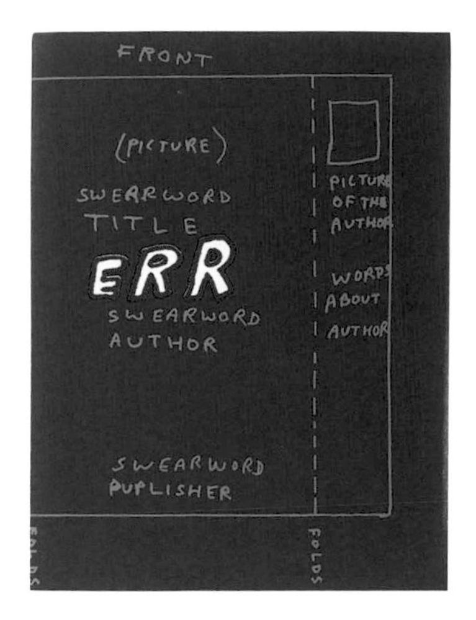

Err (1995)

96pp, 210 x 150mm, published in an edition of 1,000 copies as part of the New Writing Series, edited by Michael Bracewell and Jane Rolo; selected from open submission. Printed offset, with a soft cover.

ISBN 1 870699 22 X

Verdi Yahooda's book is in three distinct parts, but the first thing that one notices is its uncompromising reinvention of the physical form of the book. The subjects addressed by the System, as announced in the foreword, include the 'crafts' as well as the arts; but the book's preciousness is not based on rare or fine materials. Loose printed sheets, which vary slightly in their gloss and finish, are bound in manilla pattern cutter's board, held in place by metal fixings which are easily opened; though the folds of the covers, front and back are stitched with cotton thread. The cover is embossed with part of a pattern printed in reverse: the word ƎDIUӘ is just legible. It is the combination of printing and binding rarely exploited in book production with the enigma of how the parts of the book inter-relate that make the book so enticing.

That enigma is profound, and disorientating. The title's use of a definite article assures us that we will be given a guide to an actually existing state of affairs, The System; but the language of the foreword, with its surprising optimism in archaic-sounding 'progress' and 'progression', resembles that of Kafka in its ability to bedevil, and leaves one with no clear idea of the nature of the system being treated.

The first section, LANDMARKS, consists of a pattern-cutter's guide to the labelling of the parts of a woman's body for measuring purposes, and guidelines for the making of a bodice. This is illustrated with photographs of a mature woman whose eyes are masked off. The unfamiliarity of the technical language used for the parts of the body is striking. A typed table headed 'Guidelines to the System of Constructing the Bodice Block (using Direct Measures)' then locates the system that the foreword led us to think philosophical in a professional realm; and despite the apparent brutality of the language, it aims to make a universally applicable method of contriving a perfect fit for an individual. Verdi Yahooda trained as a pattern-cutter for a year and that experience informs the book; the images in this section, although they may appear to be found images, were constructed and photographed by her and her hands are doing the measuring.

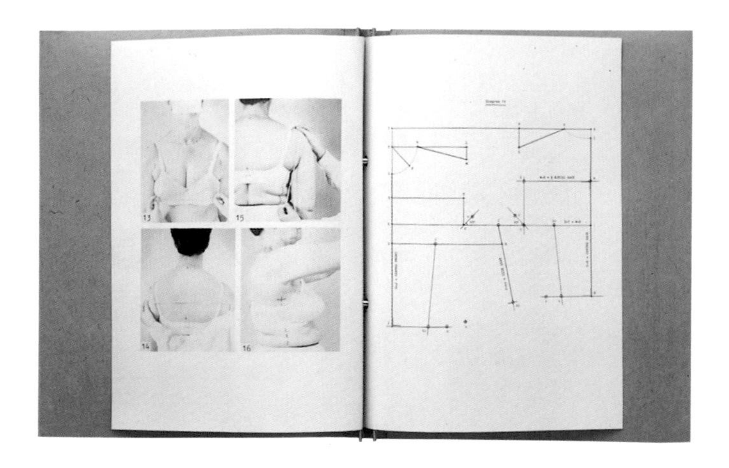

Section II is a text by Craigie Horsfield, '9th August 1990'. Yahooda's inclusion of this text in the book asks us to scrutinise it for clues to the overall 'System', while granting it its own autonomy. Its reconstruction of an event in the streets of Krakow that had occurred seventeen years previously employs a proliferation of remembered detail of buildings, tram routes and the crowd. One perception rises above all the others: the memory of a woman's ankle. 'The ankle was pale and very slightly swelling over the edge of the shoe; it was white with a film of dust and sweat but above all it was exorbitant. It filled the world . . .' This perception almost overwhelms an event one would have thought more memorable on the day in question: the death of a man under a tram. But memory obeys no measuring tape. The exorbitant ankle (though detached from its owner) speaks of life in its particularity, while the man's death is seen as an incidental and almost indifferent outcome of a city and its crowds and systems of transport.

The third section, PATHWAYS, consists of photographic images. Verdi Yahooda is, among other things, a photographer; but the progress we make to the third section has been carefully delayed. The images, multiply exposed, use long dressmaker's pins, thread, a scrap of blind-stamped paper, needles, a thimble, old-fashioned scissors. Resembling interior or perhaps mental maps, the scale and focus of the images is perplexing.

The 'pathways' are formed by pins, and the age of the metal scissors and implements locates the journey as a temporal one: an attempt to preserve or escape a past not yet grown historic. The titles and short texts that close the book retrospectively revise our understanding of the images, in the light of the deep connection of tailoring (a sedentary occupation) to storytelling: TAILOR'S TACK '*so they talk*'. It is a connection the book gathers, loose-leaf, into a precise and enigmatic contemporary form.

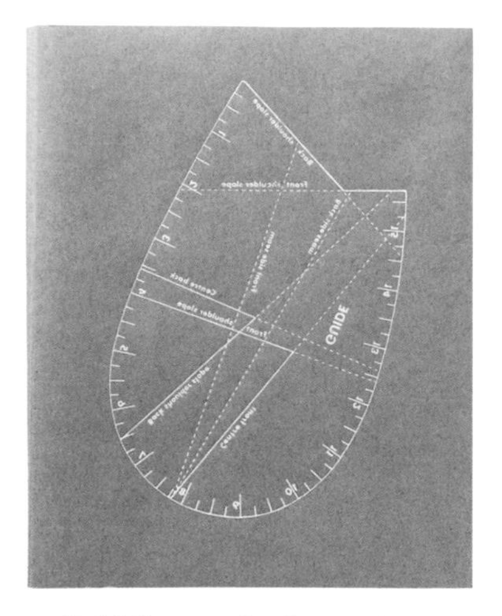

Guidelines to the System (1990)

48 pp, 220 x 170mm, published in an edition of 500 copies. Selected from open submission. The book is printed offset with a series of duotone images, presented in a pillar binding made from pattern cutting board. The cover design incorporates chalk-white blocking with hand-worked markings and perforations.

ISBN 1 870699 04 1

Silvia Ziranek has written an anthology of recipes, in part reading as an autobiographical stream of consciousness, interwoven with references to food and cooking, and introducing the reader to a witty, arch world of puns and metaphors.

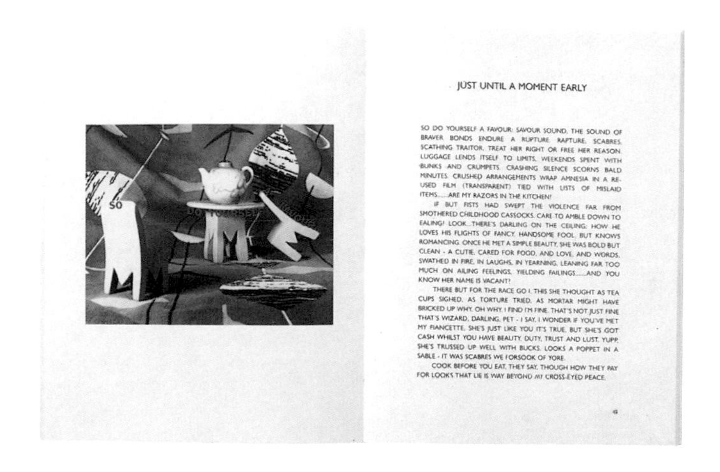

JUST UNTIL A MOMENT EARLY

SO DO YOURSELF A FAVOUR: SAVOUR SOUND, THE SOUND OF BRAVER BONDS ENDURE A RUPTURE. RAPTURE. SCABRES. SCATHING TRAITOR. TREAT HER RIGHT OR FREE HER REASON. LUGGAGE LENDS ITSELF TO LIMITS. WEEKENDS SPENT WITH BUNKS AND CRUMPETS. CRASHING SILENCE SCORNS BALD MINUTES. CRUSHED ARRANGEMENTS WRAP AMNESIA IN A RE-USED FILM (TRANSPARENT) TIED WITH LISTS OF MISLAID ITEMS......ARE MY RAZORS IN THE KITCHEN!

IF BUT FISTS HAD SWEPT THE VIOLENCE FAR FROM SMOTHERED CHILDHOOD CASSOCKS. CARE TO AMBLE DOWN TO EALING! LOOK...THERE'S DARLING ON THE CEILING: HOW HE LOVES HIS FLIGHTS OF FANCY. HANDSOME FOOL, BUT KNOWS ROMANCING. ONCE HE MET A SIMPLE BEAUTY, SHE WAS BOLD BUT CLEAN - A CUTIE. CARED FOR FOOD, AND LOVE, AND WORDS. SWATHED IN FIRE, IN LAUGHS, IN YEARNING. LEANING FAR TOO MUCH ON AILING FEELINGS, YIELDING FAILINGS......AND YOU KNOW HER NAME IS VACANT?

THERE BUT FOR THE RACE GO I. THIS SHE THOUGHT AS TEA CUPS SIGHED, AS TORTURE TRIED, AS MORTAR MIGHT HAVE BRICKED UP WHY. OH WHY. I FIND I'M FINE. THAT'S NOT JUST FINE THAT'S WIZARD. DARLING, PET - I SAY, I WONDER IF YOU'VE MET MY FIANCETTE. SHE'S JUST LIKE YOU IT'S TRUE, BUT SHE'S GOT CASH WHILST YOU HAVE BEAUTY, DUTY, TRUST AND LUST. YUPP, SHE'S TRUSSED UP WELL WITH BUCKS. LOOKS A POPPET IN A SABLE - IT WAS SCABRES WE FORSOOK OF YORE.

COOK BEFORE YOU EAT, THEY SAY, THOUGH HOW THEY PAY FOR LOOKS THAT LIE IS WAY BEYOND *MY* CROSS-EYED PEACE.

The recipes are vegetarian, 'SANS MEAT, FISH OR EGGS', and are entered as diaristic memory 'bites' which trigger off anecdotal stories and give glimpses into Ziranek's life as an artist and a cook. At the back of the book a glossary contains instructions for the recipes, which can be cooked as well as read. (This comes as something of a surprise; cookery books can sometimes feel peculiarly guilty when read with no intention of cooking anything; an art book with a practical element lacks such guilt, and may even send you off to the kitchen.) Throughout the book a certain realism punctuates the smattering of faux kitchen French, as shown by a love of 'THE BEETROOT: INTERCONTINENTAL, TOLERANT, REAL'. The recipe for Chick Pea Dip, likewise, records that bottled lemon juice is O.K. and that sesame seeds are optional, but this was 1987. The evidence that food is an area not just of snobbery, which we knew, but of fashion, is uncomfortable.

Although the predominant mood of the book is light and sly, eating and providing remain an important area of investigation and are a subtext for an analysis of consumerism, whether thoughtless, delighted or guilt-ridden: 'WE HAVE OUR CHOICE OF LABELS AND CAN CHOOSE FROM ONE OF MANY EXPLOITATIONS'. Flirtation too is an undercurrent, as it has been for previous performance art cooks such as Graham Kerr, the Galloping Gourmet. But there is no easy vault over the worktop into the audience's lap, and the effect of the speech is angular and troubling: 'AURA, DESCRIBED AS MAN, ACCUSES FOG OF ELOQUENCE.'

The book is best read aloud, as with all Ziranek's performance texts, which are printed using capital letters, a proclamatory trademark of the artist: 'TEA, GRIN OR BROIL IT DEAR? TOAST? OR FEAR? FROZEN CHEER ON ROASTED TEARS / — HEAR WHAT I MEAN.' The recipes are punctuated with images; knick-knacks, objects and fabrics from the '50s, collected and photographed by Ziranek as constructed still lives, with phrases lifted from the main texts that also begin to hint to a less light-hearted approach to life 'I JUST WON'T STORE.' 'MEATHOOKS FOR THE GROWNUPS.'

The art of eating has summoned into existence the peculiar genre of writing about eating, which has proved a versatile form. Silvia Ziranek's spin on it is challenging; beyond parody into the universe of the meta-recipe: 'INTO, INESCAPABLY, INTO THE UNDIVIDED PITS OF RESERVED SPATIAL CONSIDERATION (SERVE SCOOPWISE INTO ENDURABLE BOWL / CUP / EASY INDIVIDUALITY) AND TRAP IN THIS PARTICULAR CHOREOGRAPHY AN ABSOLUTE APROPRIATION OF YOGHURT'. But the temptation to try to imitate the richness of language and tongue-in-cheek quality of Silvia's work was perhaps more aptly dared by Derek Jarman (late artist, film-maker and gardener) who wrote in the accompanying prospectus to *Very Food*:

'Potato-faced Archimbaldo, hopeless at the culinary art, the seething, frying, broiling; but great at lighting the fires, the agas and barbercues and the great hearth itself, highway to the heart, with its flickering sacral fire, picks up Silvia's book (great, great, grandperson of Mrs.B.) and flicks through the pages. A shiver of anticipation down his vegetable spine, gooseberry eyes knowing they're on to a good nosh, finding recipes enough to toast, raises a glass in that finest of immaterial cocktails, I.K.B. Gin, Cointreau and Methylene-Blue — crying, 'Here's to Silvia !'

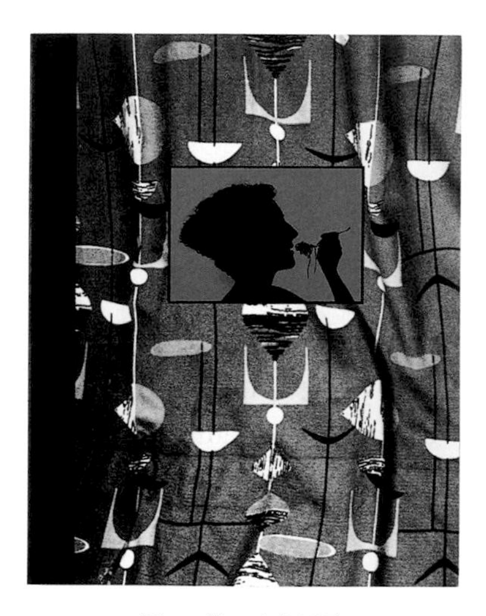

Very Food (1987)

96pp, 246 x 198mm. The book is printed offset in two colours, with soft cover and printed dust jacket. Published in an edition 750 copies, there is a special edition of 50 signed and numbered copies which includes an original screen print, and is hand bound in fifties fabric by Book Works and presented in a slip case.

ISBN 1 870699 01 7

Book Works is set up as two businesses. The studio operates as a commercial partnership, whilst the publishing and exhibition initiatives are undertaken by the limited company that is non profit-making and receives public funding from the Arts Council of England, London Arts Board and other sponsors and sources. The two businesses exist side by side in the same building, to some extent running independently of each other, but often overlapping and complementing each other.

Glyptotek
Jim Dine
Published by Pace Editions, Waddington Graphics and Jim Dine (1987-88). Edition of 90 copies. Size: 690 x 540mm. The front cover of the book was foil blocked in white with a plain black cloth slipcase. It contained 40 *glaciés tranférés* intaglio prints that were guarded into sections before sewing.

Dante's Inferno
Tom Phillips
Published by Talfourd Press (1983). Edition of 185 copies. Size: 420 x 315mm. Special binding, one of three volumes, bound at Book Works. Full vellum binding with gold blocking, screen printing and hand-stencilled lettering on spine. Cloth covered slipcase.

The studio offers a pool of resources, facilities and experience that can be drawn on, and many Book Works projects or aspects of finishing and binding are realised in practice through the studio. Book Works undertakes work for galleries, libraries, designers and a whole range of individuals, and commissioned work includes unique fine leather binding, designing and printing small editions, producing multiples, boxes and presentation portfolios. Although we specialise in hand bookbinding, box-making, and letterpress printing, many different kinds of jobs are undertaken and co-ordinated through Book Works, from simple paper binding to ornate leather presentation bindings. These are just some of the people we have undertaken work for: Eve Arnold, Dia Azzawi, Basil Beattie, David Bowie, John Cale, Ken Campbell, Brian Catling, Michael Craig-Martin, Jim Dine, Anya Gallaccio, Colin Hall, Susan Hiller, Howard Hodgkin, Tess Jaray, Derek Jarman, Nadav Kander, Sharon Kivland, Jiří Kolář, Joseph Kosuth, Ansel Krut, Yaron Livay, Adam Lowe, Ian McKeever, Nathalie Marshall Nadel, Ellis Nadler, Avis Newman, Vaughan Oliver, Tom Phillips, Paula Rego, Giorgio Sadotti, Paul Schütze, Arturo di Stefano, Glenn Sujo, John Walker, Estelle Thompson, John Wall, Kate Whiteford, Rachel Whiteread.

Ancient Proverbs
Elie Nadler
Published by Singularity Press (1988). Edition of 50 copies. Size: 460 x 340mm. The entire book was produced at Book Works Studio with the linocuts hand printed on an Atlas press. The book was bound with hand-coloured printed paper sides and a cloth spine. Cloth covered slipcase.

Tilt: the black-flagged streets
Ken Campbell
Published, printed and designed by Ken Campbell (1988). Edition of 50 copies. Size: 290 x 220mm. Bound by Book Works Studio using irregular shaped boards covered with paper printed by the artist. Spine is covered with black cloth, slipcase covered in printed paper.

Book Works tries to remain open-minded about the way in which we work with artists, and to find the best design solutions to each job that we do. Often work that is commissioned as part of the publishing programme requires an element of the production being made at the studio, and many of the more limited editions are generated this way.

For example, *Rex Reason* by Simon Patterson started off as a small hand-printed and hand-bound limited edition, which was subsequently printed offset in a much larger edition and in a smaller format.

As practitioners as well as publishers we are interested in the physical properties of the book and how the ideas contained are best communicated through every detail of its design, format and manufacture. The many cross-overs between Book Works' own commissions and the studio has also led to making works that form part of installations. For example: *Inhaled Library*, a book project by Cornelia Parker which comprised a set of unique books of rubbings by the artist taken from the exterior of Wimbledon Public Library (following her residency as Henry Moore Fellow in Sculpture at Wimbledon School of Art); the series of unique books made for Sharon Kivland's *L'attente . . . l'oubli (Book Works: A Women's Perspective)*; or the unique book produced for Brian Catling's work *The First London Halo* at The British Library, which contained a CD and hand-written texts in a binding to echo the blue leather seating and desks of the Round Reading Room. Similarly books such as those by Chris Newman, Avis Newman's *Supplement* or Brian Catling's *The Stumbling Block, its Index* take shape from collaborative discussions with the artists and are realised within the studio.

Ford Every Stream
Roy Marchant
Suspended books made by Book Works Studio forming part of an installation at Centre Point, London (1990).

This Rimy River

Vaughan Oliver

Published by 4AD/V23 (1994). Edition of 400 special copies. Size: 410 x 300mm. Binding by Book Works Studio with clear perspex covers, engraved and screen printed. Specially dyed calfskin spine, and slipcase covered in mock crushed velvet with flocked screen printing.

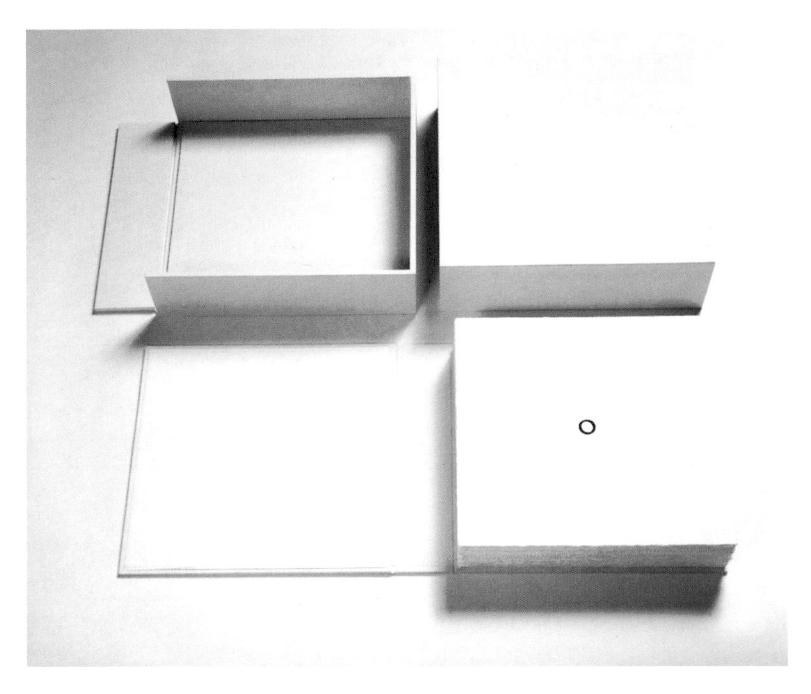

A Book of Numbers
Avis Newman

Detail of cloth-covered cases and boxes by Book Works Studio from *A Book of Numbers* (1991), a two part work consisting of the closed book displayed vertically in a vitrine, in front of a 100 inch square graphite-covered canvas. Size of print 280 x 280mm. For reference see *Vicious Circle*, catalogue of the installation at Douglas Hyde Gallery, Dublin (1993) and De Appel Foundation, Amsterdam (1993).

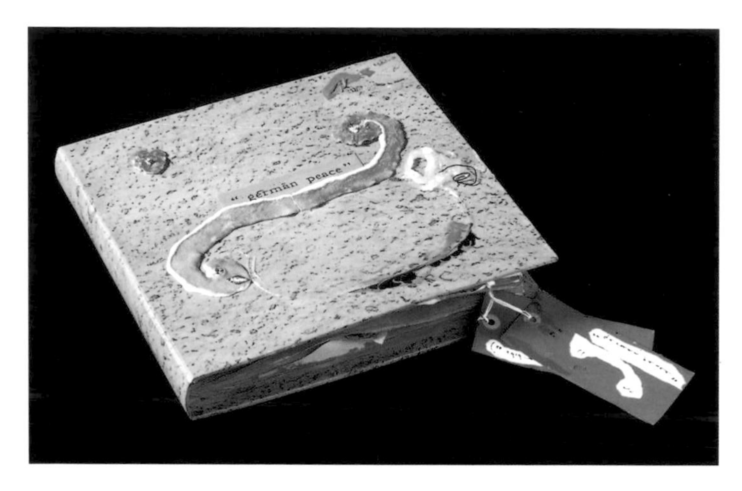

German Peace

Colin Hall

Unique book (1987). Size 290 x 310mm. Collaborative work by Colin Hall and Rob Hadrill using mixed media throughout, including orange peel on front board.

Mes Tendresses

Sharon Kivland

Multiple of 9 boxes (1995). Size: 227 x 127 x 35mm. Moiré patterned cloth covered box by Book Works Studio containing an engraved magnifying glass. The three different inscriptions on the glass were *mon coeur, mon âme,* and *mon amour.* The boxes were lined in cushioned velvet with blind blocking on the lid.

Blue

Derek Jarman

Richard Salmon Publications, original imprint Salmon, Shaw, Dane & Watson (1994). Edition of 150 copies. Size: 475 x 335mm. Printed paper covered binding by Book Works Studio, with blind embossed front cover. Drop back box covered with specially coloured blue cloth to match book.

The Goddesses, Folio 1

Madame Yevonde

Published by Yevonde Portrait Archive (1995). Edition of 30 copies. Size: 520 x 420mm. The box containing pigment transfer prints was made by Book Works Studio and has an interlocking lip on the front cover which when opened allows the box to open flat. It is covered in silk and has gold and cream coloured foil blocking with inside linings of velvet and paper. The frontispiece accompanying the prints was printed letterpress at Book Works.

Music Box

John Cale and Joseph Kosuth

Multiple produced for Carl Solway Gallery, Ohio (1994). Edition of 8. Size: 360 x 220mm. Brass musical mechanism contained inside false book made by Book Works Studio. Black boxcalf with foil-blocked panels inlaid into front cover and spine. The mechanism is mounted onto a sound box with metal fittings running through to the back cover to enhance the sound quality.

Red on Green

Anya Gallaccio

Published by the ICA, London (1994). Multiple of 40 boxes. In three different sizes from 120 x 105 x 40mm to 170 x 125 x 40mm. Paper-covered boxes by Book Works Studio with foil blocking in gold and white. Each box contains two pastels made by the artist from the ground remains of red rose blooms and stems. The roses originally formed part of an installation at the ICA in 1992.

Case containing mounted photographic transparencies for Nadav Kander

Unique case (1992). Size: 420 x 370 x 150mm. Produced at Book Works Studio in goatskin covering an aluminium frame with black cloth lining. The case opens to reveal two separate lidded compartments. Silver-plated fittings, printed labels and specially designed sprung locking system.

A Set of Etchings

Arturo di Stefano

Published by Pomeroy Purdy Print and Print Centre Publications (1992). Edition of 35 folios. Size 460 x 340mm. Cloth covered drop back box by Book Works Studio with matt and gloss black foil blocking. Frontispiece accompanying the prints printed letterpress.

Book Works has operated informally as a resource since it began, trying to offer help and encouragement to those wanting to find out more about artists' books and how to produce, publish and distribute them. Often we can best help someone by seeing them and showing them round Book Works, but as the demand increases this is not always possible, and so we've decided to produce what we hope will be a useful checklist mainly aimed at artists wanting to produce and publish books and at students interested in finding out more about the subject. We hope that some of the work featured in this book will be an inspiration in showing the diversity of styles and approaches to publishing artists' books.

SELECTION

There is no rigid policy about selection for Book Works' commissions; sometimes we will invite an artist whom we are interested to collaborate with, on other occasions artists might seek us out. At other times we might advertise for artists to send in proposals for publications selected from open submission, as in the case of our New Writing Series. Advertising of open submissions happens sporadically and not at fixed times each year, though we usually take advertisements in a national art magazines such as Art Monthly or frieze, as well as sending information to selected art and literature organisations, libraries and galleries.

Book Works also welcomes artists who wish to show us their work or discuss a particular project. Approaches can be made by post or in person at Book Works where we have one day a month specifically set aside for seeing artists' work. We are happy to advise artists about how to realise book projects but obviously have to stress we have fairly limited time and resources.

Book Works has a collection of artists' books that has grown over the years, and artists and students can arrange to look at this archive by appointment, however it has grown organically. Many of the books have been sent to us by artists as gifts and examples of their work, so the collection is for reference only, rather than a serious study collection.

COMMISSIONS

Book Works publishes about 4-5 new titles each year, and has to reject far more book proposals than it might like. However as we consider each book as a true collaboration we need to be able to concentrate our energies and financial resources in this way. Once an artist has been commissioned, a contract will be signed agreeing to terms and conditions, fees and any royalties to be paid and copyright agreements. The length of time each publication takes can vary, but often will take between one and two years to complete, with meetings mainly taking place at Book Works.

At the moment Book Works has four people working on a regular basis:

Jane Rolo (Director, Publishing and Projects), Rob Hadrill (Director, Studio, Publishing and Production), Anna Pank (Marketing, Distribution and Development), and Francis McKee (Development and Archive). We are beginning to work more with guest editors on some of our publications (Michael Bracewell, Ian Hunt). Once a book is commissioned we decide on what additional specialist help and skills are needed such as a photographer, designer, an appropriate printer or consultant, and may work with many different people on any one project.

MARKETING AND DISTRIBUTION

Book Works usually publishes the books in conjunction with a book launch to promote the work. Press releases, book lists and order forms are regularly mailed out announcing new titles. Orders can be made direct to Book Works as we currently organise our own distribution of books. We do not normally handle distribution or stock books by other publishers.

Book Works' publications are available in a variety of art bookshops and galleries in the UK, Europe and the USA, and all books carry an ISBN number (International Standard Book Number). These are unique numbers from which books, publishers and distributors can be traced through Whitaker's *Books in Print* (a full list of books published in the UK and a key information source for bookshops; available in most libraries). Specialist libraries which collect Book Works' publications include the

National Art Library at the V&A, Chelsea School of Art Library, Tate Gallery Library, Royal College of Art Library, New York Public Library, Museum of Modern Art, New York, Bibliothèque Nationale, Paris as well as many other public and private collections.

Book Works continues to participate in book fairs such as the Frankfurt Book Fair, Artistbook International and the London Artist Book Fair. As well as the larger projects, we organise small touring exhibitions of Book Works' publications and are often invited to give talks and lectures on certain aspects of artist's book publishing and production. In addition many of our publications are included in survey exhibitions and catalogues.

SELF-AUTHORISATION

IAN HUNT

Artists' books are often published from within an association of people who know one another, where the relationship between commissioner and artist may consist of friendship and support rather than a strictly commercial deal. Although there are some publishers and presses who have devoted their entire energies to artists' books, and there are many within the complex meshing of publicly supported and commercial galleries that are prepared to sometimes publish book works rather than a conventional catalogue, this informal, self-authorising sector is likely to remain the largest area of activity. It is worth looking at the nature of some of the relationships and practices involved.

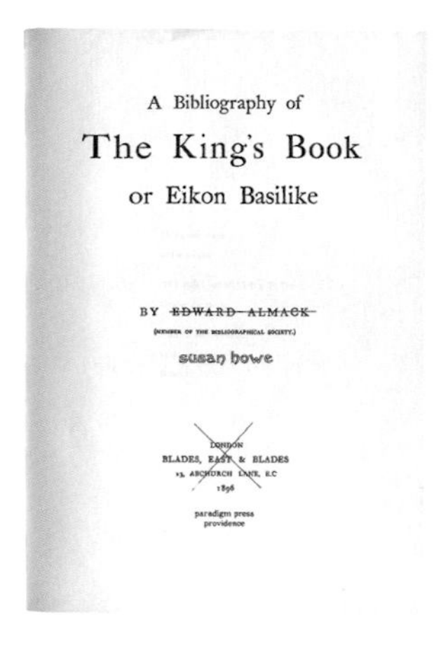
A Bibliography of

The King's Book

or Eikon Basilike

BY ~~EDWARD ALMACK~~

(MEMBER OF THE BIBLIOGRAPHICAL SOCIETY.)

susan howe

LONDON

BLADES, EAST & BLADES

23, ABCHURCH LANE, E.C

1896

paradigm press

providence

Susan Howe, *A Bibliography of The King's Book or Eikon Basilike*, Paradigm Press, Providence (1989).
Title page set by Rosemarie Waldrop.

My own knowledge of these areas is derived more from a long term interest in writing that, for many reasons, has often been published by informal networks of association rather than by orthodox publishing houses. These are the books that people thought should exist, though the possibilities for distribution of them are small. The presses often evolve out of the editing of magazines and reviews. They are written, edited, designed and sometimes typeset and printed by those who do not recognise the current capabilities of commercial publishing as a natural limit on thought. As such, although there is a distinctly different history involved, the small press sector offers some interesting analogies to questions that arise in the publishing of artists' books. And some presses have, with limited resources, published books that are striking in their format and design, and announce in their appearance a readjustment of the relationship between publisher and author, so that the choice of image, page layout and typography may contribute to the particular form of attention the text needs.

These may seem like luxuries that writers can ill afford as compared to sales and publicity, but the model of publishing as a collaborative partnership (as exemplified by Book Works' approach) has much to teach about why people persist in doing the things they do. At present the competition for space in bookshops is such that some publishers, to the frustration of their editors and authors, are making decisions on pulping based on stock movement figures from only a few months after publication. An imaginatively produced and promoted small press title, likely to be a long-term proposition for the publisher (as far as storage space permits) can sometimes seem preferable to a marketplace grown so impatient. For those unfortunate enough to write poetry it may be the only option.

Publishing, if it is to mean anything, must mean a making public and a negotiation of the practical limitations of circulation in a form that co-operates with or sometimes antagonises and questions those limitations. (It cannot be an accident that the first question sought of many small press and artists' books is the size of the edition, the place where cultural ambition and printers' bills make their accord.) The fact that publisher and producer may know one another, or sometimes be one another, need not preclude sustained thought on the book's reception and the role of design, title and accompanying publicity in that process. A purist approach may be a necessity for works that are primarily visual, where the presence of descriptive or critical blurb ('prose stigmata' as someone once described it to me) is likely to have an unwarranted influence on the reception of the book in the reader's mind and on the way in which critical thoughts about it begin to form. Such works are best promoted and framed by exhibitions, which though they may take place in a similar mixture of entrepreneurship, friendship or public patronage, are now, happily, places where this mixture does not preclude serious thought about who the likely audience is and what issues that limitation brings with it.

Negotiating minimum legal requirements (contracts with delivery dates, proportions of the edition reserved for the artist — commercial publishers allow only six copies plus the right to buy at wholesale price, for comparison) is also a good idea. Even within the parameters of goodwill and the particularities of the relationship concerned, this will focus the attention of both producer and publisher on what is sought by the act of publication: on whether the book will serve as a promotional tool for the artist or be priced in relation to what the market can support or stand.

And it should never be forgotten in all this that the book's primary function is to be scintillating, however that is to be defined. Some books by artists (Marcel Broodthaers' *A Voyage on the North Sea*, Susan Hiller's *Sisters of Menon*, Jiří Kolář's *Mode d'Emploi* . . .) have been that. And when originally issued they have the particular excitement provided by an intimate format, a direct address to the reader, and the possibility of being picked up in another continent years later and giving someone an idea. Publishing can only go so far with this process. At a certain point it is necessary to repeat the advice given by Ted Berrigan at the Jack Kerouac School of Disembodied Poetics in Boulder, Colorado: 'One way, for example, to write a terrific poem is to have every line be terrific.'[1]

1. *Talking Poetics* from the Naropa Institute, eds. Anne Waldman and Marilyn Webb, quoted in *Poets on Writing* ed. Denise Riley (London: Macmillan 1992), p.2. The book serves as an introduction to some poets in Britain who have largely been confined to the small press, self-authorising sector; a situation no longer adequately described by terms such as avant-gardism or innovation. The current crop of literary magazines emphasising prose and published in paperback or glossy format, such as *Pulp Fiction*, form another area demonstrating the kinds of audiences that small operators and individuals recognize and help to render self-conscious. To find out more about the activities of small presses and the self-authorising literary sector, the Poetry Library at London's Royal Festival Hall is a good place to start. Compendium Bookshop in Camden, London has a wide range of magazines, poetry and fiction from independent publishers and stocks US imports. Peter Riley (27 Sturton Street, Cambridge CB1 2QG) a specialist poetry bookseller, issues regular lists of secondhand poetry and small press magazines, and a critical selection and listing of what's new from current small presses; in the US a publicly supported distributor and bookstore (Small Press Distribution, Inc, 1814 San Pablo Avenue, Berkeley, CA 94702-1624; fax 510-549 2201) issues detailed critical catalogues specializing in poetry, cultural studies, art and multicultural publishing and also carries some artists' books.

SELECTED BIBLIOGRAPHY

The following information is intended as a starting point for those wishing to know more about artists' books. Many of these books include comprehensive general bibliographies

FACING THE PAGE: BRITISH ARTISTS' BOOKS, A SURVEY 1983-1993 (estamp; 1993), ISBN 1 871831 11 3. *Includes useful addresses of collections and bookshop/retail outlets as well as lists of artists' books published in the UK, 1983-93.*

THE D.A.P. ARTISTS' BOOK CATALOGUE (Distributed Art Publishers Inc., 636 Broadway, 12th Floor, New York NY 10012, 1995). *DAP/Distributed Art Publishers first catalogue devoted to artists' books and special editions from international publishers.*

WORK & TURN: ARTISTS' BOOKWORKS FROM THE UNITED KINGDOM 1980-92 (Open Editions, 1992), ISBN 0 94004 06 5. *A well produced catalogue of artists' books from the '80s and '90s.*

ARTISTS' BOOKS: THE BOOK AS A WORK OF ART, 1963-1995 (Scolar Press, 1995), ISBN 1 85928 163 X. *Useful resource book by Stephen Bury, Librarian at Chelsea College of Art, good general bibliography.*

ART UNLIMITED: MULTIPLES OF THE 1960S AND 1990S FROM THE ARTS COUNCIL COLLECTION (South Bank Centre, London, 1994).

THE ARTIST PUBLISHER: A SURVEY BY CORACLE PRESS (Crafts Council Gallery, London, 1986).

BROUGHT TO BOOK: THE BALANCE OF BOOKS AND LIFE edited by Ian Breakwell and Paul Hammond (Penguin, 1994). *An illustrated anthology of mostly original texts on the theme of books and reading, by a wide and unconventional range of writers and artists.*

THE CENTURY OF ARTISTS' BOOKS Johanna Drucker, (Granary Books, New York, 1995). *A study of the development of artists' books as a twentieth century art form, by the author of many other relevant books on typography in relation to modern art, modernism, and poetry.*

PRIVATE VIEWS AND OTHER CONTAINERS Cathy Courtney (estamp; 1992). *Reviews of artists' books from Art Monthly's regular writer on the subject.*

ARTISTS' BOOKS: A CRITICAL ANTHOLOGY AND SOURCEBOOK edited by Joan Lyons, (Visual Studies Workshop Press, Rochester NY, 1985).

PUBLISHING PHOTOGRAPHY – A PRACTICAL GUIDE edited by Dewi Lewis & Alan Ward, (Cornerhouse Publications, Manchester, 1992). *A comprehensive guide to those seeking to act as self-publishers, with useful sections on the book business and the book trade, and good advice on how to present work to potential publishers.*

TURNING OVER THE PAGES: SOME BOOKS IN CONTEMPORARY ART exhibition catalogue edited by Pavel Büchler, with short biographies (Kettles Yard Gallery, Cambridge, 1986).

ARTIST'S BOOK YEARBOOK 1996-97 edited by Tanya Peixoto, John Bently & Stephanie Brown (Magpie Press, 1996), ISBN 0 952 3880 6 5 *Information on Book Art courses and useful addresses, with reviews, interviews and articles by critics and practitioners.*

ARTIST/AUTHOR: THE ART OF THE BOOK SINCE 1980 edited by Cornelia Lauf and Clive Phillpot (American Federation of Arts & Distributed Art Publishers, forthcoming, 1997). *Critical general survey of artists' books since 1980, with good general essays.*

Bookshops and galleries dedicated to stocking artists' books and which carry wide selections:

WORKFORTHEEYETODO
51 Hanbury Street, London E1 3JP

PRINTED MATTER
77 Wooster Street, New York, NY 10012

HARDWARE GALLERY
162 Archway Road, London N6 5BB

WALTHER KÖNIG BOOKSHOP
Ehrenstrasse 4, 50672 Köln 1, Germany

Bookshops in London usually carrying a small range of artists' books (including Book Works titles): ICA, Serpentine Gallery Bookshop, Zwemmer's at Whitechapel, Camden Arts Centre, Tate Gallery, Hayward Gallery, Ian Shipley Books, Photographers Gallery, and some branches of Dillons and Waterstones.

Bookshops/gallery shops outside London include Arnolfini, IKON, Museum of Modern Art, Oxford, Tate Gallery, Liverpool, Fruitmarket Gallery, Edinburgh, CCA Glasgow, Cornerhouse, Manchester, Minories Colchester, and again a few branches of Dillons and Waterstones.

There are so many different methods of production, print and design that it is well worth looking at a lot of books before embarking on publishing or self-publishing an artist's book. Libraries and collections should be sought out, while bookshops provide an opportunity to see the range on sale, but also to see the effectiveness of presentation, packaging and how artists' books are shelved. For example at workfortheeyetodo artists' books are grouped by publisher on the shelves, or displayed flat on tables, whereas in a more general art bookshop such as the ICA titles may be organised under individual artists' names or given display space on the wall, with covers facing out. Equally important is deciding on retail prices for the edition, a factor which can effect dramatically how well a book may sell. It is certainly worth seeing how prices can affect the size and scale of an edition.

FUNDING AND SOURCES OF MONEY; SELF-PUBLISHING

There are still relatively few sources of funding specifically for artists' books. However the Arts Council of England's Visual Arts Department has three funds currently that will consider them: Visual Arts Publications, Photography Publications and First Time Publications. The grants offered will help subsidise the costs to some extent, but publishers are still expected to generate an income through book sales, a fact that needs to be considered carefully in planning a budget.

Regional Arts Boards may also provide funding for some publications, as will many universities and colleges which may have research grants available for publishing projects, and have changed their attitudes to publishing in general as a result of the changes to the system of research rating. There are also independent trusts and foundations which support visual art and education activities, such as the Paul Hamlyn Trust and the Elephant Trust, which have supported the publication of artists' books.

1984

CROCODILE PUDDLES May - June
A collaborative book by Christian Hasucha, Rob Hadrill and Roger McGough, with other works by Christian Hasucha.

THE RUINED BOOK July - August
An installation by Langlands & Bell.

ARTIFACTS AT THE END OF A DECADE August - September
A collective book work by 45 American artists, including Laurie Anderson, Futura 2000, Robert Wilson and Sol LeWitt, curated by Steve Watson.

BEST OF THE YEAR October - November
Recent book works by students, selected by David Sellars and Vanessa Marshall.

BOOK WORKS CHRISTMAS SHOW December - January
A selection of contemporary artists' books.

1985

WATER LEAVES AND OTHER FOLIOS February - March
New works by Ian Tyson.

DAVID SELLARS AND KEN CAMPBELL March - April
The bindings of David Sellars and the printed books and sculptures of Ken Campbell.

THREE BOOK ARTISTS May - June
Susan Share, Kay Hines and Jenny Leimert, and a performance *Unfolding* by Susan Share.

Player-Typewriter-Roll-Blues Book
Kay Hines
Three Book Artists (1985)

FRIENDS OF BOOK WORKS SHOW September - October
A selection of contemporary artists' books.

CIRCLE PRESS PUBLICATIONS AND WORK FROM THE RUINS October - November
Ron King (Circle Press), Hannah Vowles, Glyn Banks and John Coleman (Art in Ruins).
A selection of books by Ron King's Circle Press and the launch of *Work from Common Knowledge* published by Circle Press; *From The Ruins* an installation with Hannah Vowles, Glyn Banks and John Coleman.

SUSAN JOHANKNECHT December - January
Recent book works by Susan Johanknecht, and a selection of artists' books including work by Liver & Lights, Writers Forum, Natalie d'Arbeloff, Hangman Books and Woolley Dale Press.

1986

edition hansjörg mayer April - May
In conjunction with Nigel Greenwood books.
An exhibition of books by edition hansjörg mayer,
including books by Dieter Rot, Liliane Lijn, Tom Phillips and Richard Hamilton.

THE FOUR ELEMENTS
Brighton Festival (May),
Milton Keynes Exhibition Gallery (November - December) & City Museum and Art Gallery, Hanley (April 1987).
New commissioned work by Denys Blacker, Susan Hiller, Gary F. Miller, Keir Smith, and Richard Wilson.
A catalogue was published by Book Works and Milton Keynes Exhibition Gallery in an edition of 500 copies.

Performance in Borough Market
Richard Layzell
Site Works I (1986)

SITE WORKS I October
Commissioned work in and around Borough Market by Langlands & Bell, Richard Layzell, Cornelia Parker.
Film by Langlands and Bell.
Performance and drawings by Richard Layzell.
Sculpture and installations by Cornelia Parker.

THE WALL installation and new book by Pavel Büchler *2200th Anniversary of the Great Wall of China, Berlin 1961-1986* and an exhibition of artists' books from Book Works catalogue (November - December).

1987

BOOK WORKS (LONDON)
Center for Book Arts, New York (April - May) and University of Toledo, Ohio (June - August)
New work by Langlands and Bell.
Work by Romilly Saumarez Smith, Pella Erskine-Tulloch, Jane Rolo, Rob Hadrill, Nicholas Phillips, David Sellars, Susan Johanknecht, Ken Campbell, Jake Tilson and David Jacobson.

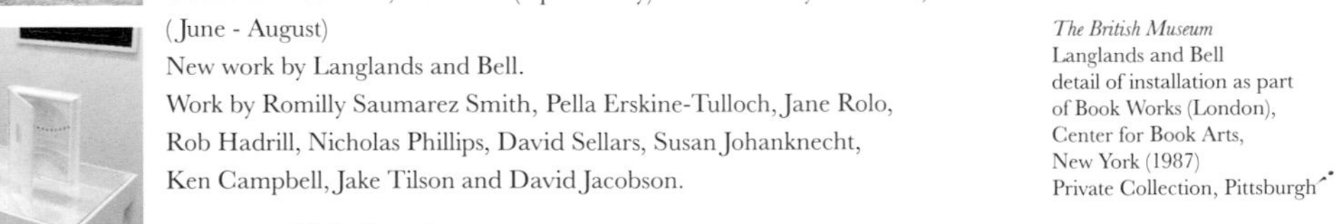

The British Museum
Langlands and Bell
detail of installation as part of Book Works (London), Center for Book Arts, New York (1987)
Private Collection, Pittsburgh

VERY FOOD Silvia Ziranek
Exhibition and performance tour to launch the publication of *Very Food, 1987-88*
Nigel Greenwood Gallery, Plymouth Arts Centre, Link Centre, Swindon, Central Library, Brighton (and performances at the Royal Pavilion, Brighton, Third Eye Centre, Glasgow).

STORY OF A FINE BINDING
Royal Festival Hall, London and tour 1987-88
An exhibition about the construction of a book, with photography by Verdi Yahooda.

1988

Book in a Jar (April 9 1984)
Colin Hall
unique book, sour milk,
German sketch book/diary wi
fermenting rice, Book Works a
the V&A, (1988)
National Art Library, V&A
Museum Collection

BOOK WORKS AT THE V&A February - April
Art in Ruins: Glyn Banks & Hannah Vowles, Ed Baxter, Ken Campbell, Brian Catling, Colin Hall & Rob Hadrill, Susan Johanknecht and Katharine Meynell, Kurt Johannessen, Lucia King, Knife Edge Press (Bruce McLean & Mel Gooding), and Silvia Ziranek.

SITE WORKS II April
Brian Catling, Jo Stockham, Stefan Szcelkun.
Skyline, performance and publication by Stefan Szcelkun.
For Wealth Work Woe, an installation using sound and image by Jo Stockham.
Under A Stone Wheel, performance by Brian Catling.

1990

JOURNEY OF A BOOK October - December
Book Works at the British Library
Journey of a Book an exhibition that looks at techniques and processes used in making artists' books, featuring *Meeting in the Middle*, a new book by Les Bicknell, with photographs by Vince Bevan.
And books by Pavel Büchler, Ken Campbell, Brian Catling, Circle Press, Sheila Clark, Natalie D'Arbeloff, Gefn Press, Bruce McLean & Mel Gooding, Chris Newman, Jake Tilson, and Verdi Yahooda.

Notable Days
Pavel Büchler
installation at
Princelet Street,
London (1990)

BOOK WORKS NEW WORK 1990 November
Installations at 4 Princelet Street, Spitalfields, London E1
Notable Days by Pavel Büchler, *Stony Air* by Brian Catling, *Pathways* by Verdi Yahooda to accompany the launch of their three new books.
Performance *Stony Ground* by Brian Catling at The Crypt, St George's Church, Bloomsbury, London.

1992

BOOK WORKS: A WOMEN'S PERSPECTIVE March - April
CITY OF LONDON POLYTECHNIC
An international conference addressed the subject, *Book Works: A Women's Perspective*, looking at the issues raised and the problems surrounding production and publication of books and texts in recent years, through a series of papers, artists' presentations and discussions.

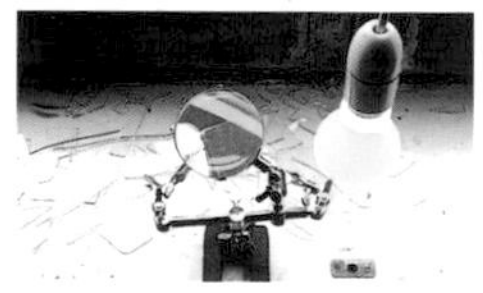

Notable Days
Pavel Büchler
detail from installation,
magnifying glass with
section of Berlin Wall

Speakers included Rita Keegan (chair), Hilary Robinson, Joan Lyons, Deborah Sugg, the Guerilla Girls, Caroline Bergvall, Marysia Lewandowska, Adrian Piper, Susan Johanknecht, Katharine Meynell, and Ulrike Stoltz.
Performances and poetry readings by Jean Binta Breeze, Maya Chowdhry, and intermittent appearances by Fanny Adams and the Guerilla Girls.

Book Works: A Women's Perspective exhibition New Loom House, London (1992) general view of exhibition, with detail of hanging text by Tracey Emin *'This is Sincerely Mine'*

NEW LOOM HOUSE, LONDON - exhibition

The exhibition featured artists' books and book works by women, and offered a visual accompaniment to the conference, illustrating ways in which women have used the book form in their work.

Artists included: Kathy Acker, Caroline Bergvall, Barbara Bloom, Sheila Burnett & Deborah Levy, Sophie Calle, Maya Chowdhry, Johanna Drucker, Tracey Emin, the Guerilla Girls, Denise Hawrysio, Jenny Holzer, Erica van Horn, Els ter Horst, Maria Jastrzebska & Jola Scicinska, Susan Johanknecht & Katharine Meynell, Mary Kelly, Sharon Kivland, Barbara Kruger, Marysia Lewandowska, Joan Lyons, Lily R. Markiewicz, Tanya Peixoto, Adrian Piper, Mary Plant, Ingrid Pollard, Unica T, Visual Studies Workshop, Verdi Yahooda, Silvia Ziranek.

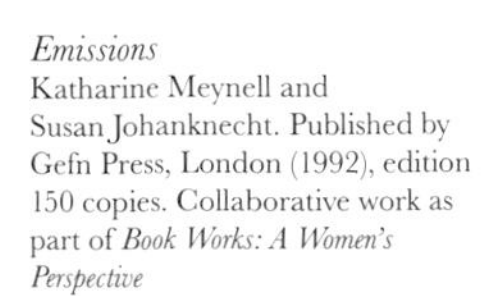

Emissions
Katharine Meynell and Susan Johanknecht. Published by Gefn Press, London (1992), edition 150 copies. Collaborative work as part of *Book Works: A Women's Perspective*

A Will for Land
Caroline Bergvall
a multi-media performance presentation as part of conference for *Book Works: A Women's Perspective*

Installations - *L'attente . . . l'oubli* by Sharon Kivland, *Places to Remember* by Lily R. Markiewicz, and collaborative commissions - *No More Utopias* by Sheila Burnett and Deborah Levy, and *Emissions* by Susan Johanknecht and Katharine Meynell.

1993

COLLECTED WORKS January - March

National Art Library, Victoria and Albert Museum

Reading Matter, an installation by Cornelia Parker, and launch of new publication *Lost Volume: A Catalogue of Disasters.*

Time Piece, a live work by Gary Stevens.

Selection of work by all the artists in library.

Celebrating the Art of the Book - talk by Jan van der Wateren, Chief Librarian, National Art Library.

Central Library, Kensington

Happy Families, an installation by John Paul Bichard.

Jackie Kay - reading from *The Year of the Letter*, commissioned by Book Works, at Brompton Library and North Kensington Library.

installations - Raul Speek

Chelsea Library

The Phone Box, Art in Telephone Boxes - publication and installations curated by Virginia Nimarkoh and featuring work by Tracey Emin, David Fryer, Sher Rajah and Damien Robinson.

Happy Families
John Bichard
an installation in the Central Library, Kensington as part of *Collected Works* (1993)

Happy Families
John Bichard
detail of text work as part of installation, vinyl hand-cut texts

1994

THE READING ROOM March - May

London, Oxford, Glasgow.

The Writers' Reading Room was shown at Camden Arts Centre (London), Transmission Gallery (Glasgow) and Museum of Modern Art (Oxford) and comprised *Getting Shallow* by Michael Bracewell, *The Year of the Letter* by Jackie Kay and *Reading Rooms* by Janice Galloway, with readings in Glasgow and Oxford.

Scroll
Brian Catling
detail of installation in performance at The British Library, *The Reading Room* (199

London
Mysteries of the heart by Susan Brind and Jim Harold (Camden Arts Centre).
The Reading Room a programme of videos curated by Breda Beban and Hrvoje Horvatic (Camden Arts Centre).
Susan Hiller at the Freud Museum (Freud Museum).
A Casting, The First London Halo, an installation and *Scroll*, a performance, both by Brian Catling (The British Library, Reading Room and King's Library).
Cyber Books: Read Only Memories, lecture by Sean Cubitt (Slade School of Art).

Glasgow
Silencium by Lothar Baumgarten (Transmission Gallery).
Conservatory by Lothar Baumgarten (Royal Botanic Garden, Edinburgh).
Reading Room Symposium (organised in association with Glasgow School of Art and Tramway at Partick Burgh Hall). Speakers included: Susan Brind, Pavel Büchler, Paul Crowther, Thomas Doherty, Terry Eagleton, Janice Galloway, Joseph Kosuth, Stuart Morgan, Nikos Papastergiadis, Martha Rosler, Sarat Maharaj.

Oxford
Something between my mouth and your ear by Douglas Gordon (Dolphin Gallery, St John's College).
The (Ethical) Space of Cabinets 7 & 8 by Joseph Kosuth (Voltaire Room, Taylor Institution Library).
Say: I Do Not Know by Joseph Kosuth (Divinity School, Bodleian Library).
Consider the Lilies by Elaine Reichek (Ruskin School of Drawing).
The Mound, a durational performance by Brian Catling (Oxford Castle Mound).

READING THE BOOK April
An exhibition of contemporary artists' books.
Centre for Oxfordshire Studies, Central Library, Oxford and touring in Oxfordshire 1994-95. Tour continued to Bath Central Library (Bath Literary Festival), Cleveland Arts Centre, and Sunderland City Library and Arts Centre (1995).

1995

CORACLE & BOOK WORKS NEW BOOKS FROM LONDON November
An exhibition at Printed Matter, New York.
Featuring *The Unveiling of Two Vitrines* by Paul Etienne Lincoln.

1996

ITINERANT TEXTS April 1996 -
Dartington College of Arts (April), Tramway (November), Camden Arts Centre (November-January 1997) and touring as part of *Artist/Author: The Art of the Book Since 1980* in the USA and Europe (1997), organised by the American Federation of Arts.

12 artists are involved in this project: Judith Barry, Robert Barry, Angela Bulloch, Tacita Dean, Jimmie Durham, Tracey Emin, Liam Gillick, Douglas Gordon, Susan Hiller, Joseph Kosuth, Tracy Mackenna and Simon Patterson.

BOOK WORKS
A PARTIAL HISTORY AND SOURCEBOOK

Book Works would like to thank all the artists who have published books with us, and all who have taken part in exhibitions and events over the years. This publication is a record of those many fruitful collaborations.

The book is the product of much discussion within and without Book Works, that has informed what we have written. Although most of the sections are by one or other of us, we did not want to scatter our names throughout the book. In the last stretch we swapped the approximate roles we'd had with Jane Rolo writing entries for the published works section on Sharon Kivland, Chris Newman and Silvia Ziranek, and Ian Hunt contributing to the section on artists' books and publishing. We would like to thank Pavel Büchler, Ann Gallagher and Michael Bracewell for their contributions, and some of the artists for original texts, Orna Frommer-Dawson and her assistant Geoff Windram for designing and typesetting the book, and to all at Book Works for their tolerance of us while the book has been put together.

Jane Rolo and Ian Hunt 1996

PHOTOGRAPHY CREDITS

Jeremy Ackerman, Vince Bevan, Susan Brind, The British Library, Pavel Büchler, David Cripps, Joëlle Depont, Eagle Gallery, Pella Erskine-Tulloch, Janice Galloway, Chris Guy, Nadav Kander, Stephen White, Alex Wilson and Edward Woodman — thank you all for your contributions to this book.

ACKNOWLEDGMENTS

There are many individuals who have been involved with Book Works over the years whom we would like to mention.

First of all, we would like to acknowledge and thank Pella Erskine-Tulloch, a former founder Director, who was involved with every aspect of the organisation until recently. This book is very much a record of what we achieved together from those early days.

Thanks to Jen Lindsay, Vanessa Marshall, Richard Minsky,.Tom Phillips who also helped shape Book Works in the early years.

Thanks to those who have worked at the studio, in particular Jessica Ahmon, Nic Gardner, Alex Rodgers, Monique Wass and Ann Zwemmer and to Anna Pank for all her work in helping to promote Book Works.

And thanks to all those involved with Book Works projects: Sue Brind, Katrina Brown, Ben Hillwood-Harris, Jane Carr, Colin Wight, Cornelia Lauf, Kaatje Cusse, Mary Lemley, James Brook, Simon Cutts, Erica van Horn, Vivienne Newport, Elaine Reichek, Sophie Stannard, Lisa Haskel, Vera Wallace-Hadrill, Stephen Graham, Crispin Rose-Innes, Grita van der Bend, John Cole, Dave Andrews, Paul Khera, Erica Davies, Giles Barber, Amanda King, Tim Eastop, Eileen Daly, Elizabeth Sell, John Hampson, Stephen Beddoe, Holly Tebbutt, Mariam Sharp, Diane Volckaerts, Libertad Cabielles.

In addition we would like to thank all the editors, designers, photographers, and printers who have helped us realise the projects, all the people working in galleries, bookshops and libraries who have promoted our work, and all the funders who have supported Book Works.